Understanding Named, Automatic, and **Additional Insureds** *in the CGL Policy*

Dwight M. Kealy
Attorney at Law
MA, JD, CIC

First Edition

Copyright © 2014 Dwight M. Kealy / Dwight Kealy and Associates, LLC.

All rights reserved.

ISBN: 978-0-578-14537-2

This text is provided for educational purposes only. The author will not provide legal or other professional advice unless agreed to in writing, in advance. Insurance matters may be complicated and you need to discuss the specific facts of your cases with an appropriate advisor.

This book may be eligible for Continuing Education Credit from the Department of Insurance in your state.

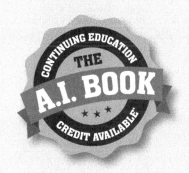

1. **Go to: www.GoGetCE.com**
2. **Pass the Quiz**
3. **Get Insurance Continuing Education Credits**

Dwight Kealy is an attorney, author, and insurance coverage analyst based in Southern California. Dwight graduated from high school in Quito, Ecuador, earned his B.A. from Westmont College in Santa Barbara, California, studied archaeology in Israel with Harvard University, earned his master's degree from Yale University, and served as an Intelligence Analysis Officer in the United States Marine Corps. After all of this, Dwight found that insurance was the perfect fit for his interest in helping people analyze and reduce their risks. Now, instead of looking at ancient maps or military risks, Dwight helps businesses address the financial and legal risks that they face every day.

Dwight is a licensed insurance producer who spent more than a decade in the commercial insurance industry where he was Chief Operating Officer/Vice President for one of California's largest insurance agencies for contractors' liability insurance. Dwight is a Certified Insurance Counselor and Faculty Member with the National Alliance for Insurance Education and Research where he teaches commercial casualty classes. Dwight is a member of the American Bar Association's Forum on the Construction Industry and the American Bar Association's Tort Trial and Insurance Practice Section. He lives in Southern California with his wife, two children, and lab/great-dane dog.

Contents

Introduction

Every day, thousands of people request and receive proof of someone else's Commercial General Liability (CGL) insurance. They might be named as a certificate holder or they might be named as an additional insured. They might want to be named as an additional insured for ongoing operations, completed operations, or "your work." They might request Primary Wording, or Non-Contributory Wording, or a Waiver of Subrogation, or a Hold Harmless Agreement. They might say that the insurance company has to have an A.M. Best Rating of at least A-, VIII, and write business in the state on an admitted basis. **WHAT DOES ALL OF THIS MEAN?**

Who is an Insured?

The point of an additional insured endorsement is to modify the policy to add an individual or entity as an insured that is not already insured by the policy. If an individual or entity is already an insured, then it may not make sense to go through the effort to endorse the policy to name someone as an additional insured who is already insured by the policy. Therefore, before discussing additional insureds, we need to start by looking at who is an insured under the CGL policy without an additional insured endorsement. All CGL policies have a Section called, "Who is an Insured." The first paragraph in the section discusses the **Named Insureds**. The second paragraph discusses the **Automatic Insureds**.

The Named Insured (Section II, 1. A-E)

I hope that it is not a surprise to you that the person or entity named as the insured in the declarations of the insurance policy is, in fact, an insured in the policy. The CGL policy identifies the following types of individuals or entities that may be named as insureds: individuals, partnerships, joint ventures, limited liability companies, organizations (corporations), and trusts.

If an <u>individual</u> is listed as the insured in the declarations, that individual is an insured. This individual's spouse is also an insured, but only with respect to the conduct of a business of which the individual is a sole owner.

For example: If an individual named Jill Johnson has a business and gets a policy with her name as the insured, then Jill Johnson is the named insured on the policy. Jill Johnson's spouse is also covered by the policy, but only with respect to the conduct of a business. Imagine that Jill has a coffee shop. Her husband Joe goes to a coffee convention where he is demonstrating their new coffee bean grinder. Unfortunately, it is not a very good coffee bean grinder. It starts a fire and damages the room hosting the coffee convention. If Joe is named on a lawsuit connected to this fire, he should have coverage under Jill Johnson's CGL policy because the policy names her as an individual, Joe is her spouse, and the occurrence arose with respect to the conduct of Jill's coffee business.

If a partnership is listed in the declarations as the insured, the named partnership, all partners and spouses of partners are insured, but only with respect to the conduct of the business.

If a joint venture is listed in the declarations as the insured, the named joint venture, all members of the joint venture and spouses of the members are insured, but only with respect to the conduct of the business.

If a limited liability company is listed in the declarations as the insured, the named limited liability company, its members, and its managers are insured, but only with respect to their duties as the limited liability company's managers.

Notice that although there was automatic coverage for spouses with respect to the conduct of the business for named individuals, partnerships, and joint ventures, spouses are not automatically included with the limited liability company.

If an organization (Corporations) is listed in the declarations as the insured, the named entity, the executive officers, directors, and stockholders are insured, but only with respect to their liability in these roles.

For example: You could take a break from reading this book to buy one share of stock in a large automobile corporation of your choosing. As a stockholder, you are a part owner of that corporation. Your one share will give you one vote in the next election for company directors. The directors then hire the executive officers who implement the decisions made by the Board of Directors. If in three years we learn that the new car the company makes suddenly explodes after three years, you can imagine that there are probably a number of car owners who might sue the company looking for compensation. The corporation, the executive officers, and directors are all covered under the CGL policy. You are also covered under the automobile manufacturer's CGL policy if you are named in the lawsuit with respect to liability you might have as a stockholder. Why might you be dragged into the lawsuit? Well, you did vote for the director who hired the executive officer who implemented the company's decisions. You can imagine that this provision becomes more important when there is a wealthy shareholder who owns a significant amount of a privately held corporation, and someone is trying to sue those responsible for the corporation's actions. The wealthy stockholder may be sued because she or he is a stockholder even though the stockholder is not a director or executive officer. The CGL policy would provide a defense for this wealthy stockholder for liability arising out of his/her role as stockholder.

If a trust is listed in the declarations as the insured, the named trust is insured. Trustees are also insured, but only with respect to their duties as trustees.

The Automatic Insureds (Section II, 2 & 3)

In addition to the named insureds listed above, the CGL policy acknowledges that there are certain individuals or entities that should be granted automatic insured status because of their close relationship with the named insured. These include Employees and Volunteer Workers of the named insured, Real Estate Managers, Legal Representatives when the named insured Dies, and Newly Acquired Organizations.

Employees and Volunteer Workers are covered under the CGL policy, but only for acts within the scope of their employment or while performing duties related to the conduct of the business. These workers are not covered if they cause bodily injury or property damage to the named insured. This is because liability policies, in general, are looking to provide coverage for bodily injury or property damage to others; not to an insured. If the named insured is looking for coverage for his or her own property, then the named insured needs to purchase a property policy that will cover his or her own property. Liability Insurance is designed to pay for bodily injury or property damage *to others*.

Any person acting as a Real Estate Manager for the named insured is also an automatic insured. **For example**: Imagine that the named insured is an entity that owns an apartment building. You agree to be the Real Estate Manager for this entity in exchange for free rent. You collect the monthly rent from all of the other tenants and you think everything is fine until you get sued by one of the tenants because of something they think you did or should have done in connection with being the real estate manager. You would be an automatic insured under the apartment's CGL policy because you are a Real Estate Manager for the named insured.

If the named insured dies, any person or organization having proper temporary custody of the named insured's property is an automatic insured with respect to liability arising out of the maintenance or use of that property. This coverage ends when a legal representative has been appointed for the now deceased named insured.

Newly Acquired Organizations. If there is no other policy in place, there is temporary automatic coverage for corporations that the named insured acquires or forms. The coverage extends for 90 days or until the end of the policy period, whichever is earlier. The new entity is an automatic insured so long as the named insured has a majority ownership interest in the new entity. This automatic coverage does not apply to Partnerships, Joint Ventures, or Limited Liability Companies.

Who is NOT an Insured (Section II, Final Paragraph)

After describing the named insured and automatic insureds as described above, the policy ends the "Who is an Insured" section with a statement to clarify who is not an insured.

No person or organization is an insured with respect to the conduct of any current or past partnership, joint venture or limited liability company that is not shown as a named insured in the declarations.

At first glance this seems reasonable and should not surprise anyone. If you are not a named insured and you are not an automatic insured, you probably should not expect to be covered by the policy unless you have coverage from an "insured contract" (discussed below), or if you have been specifically added as an additional insured to the policy by endorsement. However, as with any time in life when you tell people what they do not want to hear, there tends to be confusion on the topic of who is an insured when you tell someone that he or she is not covered by an insurance policy. This is especially true when the person paying for the policy is not covered by the policy. How can it happen that the person paying for the insurance policy is not a named or automatic insured?

Business owners, almost by definition, tend to be entrepreneurial. They have already established one business that is insured. What makes you think that they are going to stop at one business? A characteristic of many entrepreneurs is that they are creative. Many of the successful ones may also be creative in limiting their expenses. With this in mind, below are some examples of when the person paying for insurance might not be covered by the policy.

Example 1:

Jones Roofing, Inc. is the named insured. The owner is Judy Jones. In addition to Jones Roofing, Inc., Judy Jones also does business as Jones General Contracting, Jones Remodeling, and Jones Deli and Pizza. In the past she had her insurance in the name of Jones General Contracting, but now the only entity with insurance is Jones Roofing, Inc.

There is an occurrence during the policy period that causes bodily injury or property damage. A lawsuit is filed against Jones General Contracting. There is no coverage under the policy for Jones General Contracting. Jones General Contracting is not the named insured and Jones General Contracting is not an automatic insured. If Judy Jones was named individually on the lawsuit, she would be covered as an automatic insured if the lawsuit was filed with respect to her liability as an Executive Officer, Director, or Stockholder of the named insured.

Example 2:

Jones' Pub and Pizza is the named insured. The owner is John Jones. This policy is the only policy John has for his business activities. It turns out that Jones' Pub and Pizza is a great venue for small concerts. John forms John Jones' Concerts, LLC. He uses this entity to coordinate with a number of bands that perform at Jones' Pub and Pizza. One night, during a concert at Jones' Pub and Pizza, someone is injured. This person files a lawsuit against John Jones' Concerts, LLC. John Jones sends the lawsuit to his insurance company and learns that there is no coverage for John Jones' Concerts, LLC.

"Why not?" He argues. "I am John Jones and I pay the premiums for this policy. I am the Jones in "Jones' Pub and Pizza!"

The answer, of course, is that the named insured is Jones' Pub and Pizza. This entity is covered as the named insured, but Jones' Pub and Pizza, the named insured, is not named in the lawsuit. John Jones' Concerts, LLC is named in the lawsuit. John Jones would be an automatic insured as the owner of Jones' Pub and Pizza, but John Jones was not named in the lawsuit. Remember, John Jones' Concerts, LLC was named in the lawsuit. John Jones' Concerts, LLC is NOT the named insured, and is not an automatic insured. Even though it contains the name John Jones in its entity name, John Jones' Concerts, LLC is NOT an entity covered by the policy for Jones' Pub and Pizza.

Insureds under an "Insured Contract"

Although not technically called an "insured" in the policy, **third-parties may have their defense costs paid by a named insured's insurance policy if the obligation to pay the defense costs arise out of an "insured contract".** When I talk about third parties, you can think of a motorcycle's sidecar. The sidecar has no ability on its own to steer or power the motorcycle. It just hangs on and the motorcycle's front and rear wheels provide steering and power for the sidecar's third wheel. The third wheel may feel vulnerable to the steering and power choices made by the other two wheels.

In insurance, the first two parties are the named insured and the Insurance Company. These are the two parties that either promised to pay premiums or promised to provide insurance coverage. They power and steer the contract. Anyone else is a third party trying to attach itself to the contract like a sidecar attaches to a motorcycle.

Although we have not jumped into talking about additional insureds, you can imagine that one of the reasons why an entity would want to be named as an additional insured is because they are a third party that wants their defense costs paid by the named insured. The third party might fear that they will be dragged into a lawsuit because of the actions of the named insured, and the third party might think that it needs to be named as an additional insured in order to get a defense from the named insured's insurance company. It may not be necessary to get the additional insured endorsement if all you want is a defense when you consider that third-parties may have their defense costs paid by a named insured's insurance policy if the obligation to pay the defense costs arise out of an "insured contract".

For example: Imagine that you have a catering business. You have been hired to cater a wedding that is going to take place at a hotel. The hotel wants to be named as an additional insured on the caterer's policy in case a hotel guest is injured by the caterer and sues the hotel. The hotel is not a named insured on the caterer's policy and the hotel is not an automatic insured (discussed above). In order for the hotel to be covered under the caterer's policy, it is common to have the caterer name the hotel as an additional insured on the caterer's policy. However, I just mentioned that third-parties may have their defense costs paid by the named insured's insurance policy if the obligation to pay the defense costs arises out of an "insured contract". This would imply that if the hotel had an "insured contract" with the caterer, the hotel could have its defense costs paid by the caterer's insurance policy without the hotel having to be named as an additional insured on the caterer's insurance policy.

It is important to note that we did not say that the caterer's policy would provide the defense for the Hotel. This is what may happen if the Hotel was named as an additional insured on the caterer's policy. We said that the caterer's policy would pay the defense costs for the hotel. This means that if the provisions of the "insured contract" are satisfied, the hotel could engage its own attorneys to defend itself rather than having to depend on the caterer's insurance to provide the defense. In order to see whether or not the hotel (or any third party) would be made whole by the "insured contract" provision, we need to understand the definition of an "insured contract", and then see what the insurance company will pay in connection with an "insured contract".

What is an "Insured Contract"?

The CGL policy excludes all contractual liability unless the liability results from an "insured contract". If the liability results from an "insured contract", then the policy may pay for the third party's attorney fees, litigation expenses, and defense costs IF these expenses were assumed in the "insured contract".

A little trick for understanding policies is the use of quotation marks in an insurance policy. These are not used for irony or emphasis. The quotation marks are used in an insurance policy to designate that the word or words within the quotation marks are defined elsewhere in the policy. Therefore, when we read that an "insured contract" is not excluded, we need to go to the definitions section to find the definition of an "insured contract".

The CGL policy defines an "insured contract" as including the following six kinds of contracts:

a)   Lease of Premises

For example: A landlord might require a tenant to hold the landlord harmless in the event that a customer is injured in the tenant's office and then sues the building owner.

6

b) Sidetrack Agreement

This is an agreement with a railroad company to accept liability associated with a railroad spur connected to your business location.

c) Easement/License Agreement

For our purposes, an easement or license agreement is similar to a lease except that the lease allows one to take possession and occupy a premise, and the easement or license agreement allows one to enter, use, or access the property of another person.

d) An Obligation as required by ordinance to indemnify a municipality.

For example: A city ordinance might require that businesses take care of the sidewalks in front of the business and to hold the city harmless in the event that someone sues the city as a result of getting injured on the sidewalk.

e) Elevator Maintenance Agreement

For example: If you have an elevator in your building, you may have to sign an Elevator Maintenance Agreement.

f) Tort Liability Assumed by the Named Insured

A tort is a civil wrong. The most common tort for insurance matters is the tort of negligence. One can be found negligent if the person had a duty to act like a reasonable person, breached the duty to act like a reasonable person, and this breach caused damages. When would one assume tort liability by contract? The most common examples relating to insurance are Hold Harmless Agreements and Indemnification Agreements.

What is a Hold Harmless Agreement?

A Hold Harmless Agreement is an agreement where one party agrees to hold another party harmless for any liabilities associated with the agreement.

What is an Indemnification Agreement?

In contract law, to indemnify means to make the other party to a contract "whole." The indemnitor gives the promise to make someone else whole. The indemnitee receives the promise to be made whole. In the indemnification agreement, the indemnitor agrees to indemnify (or make whole) the indemnitee.

Hold Harmless and Indemnification Example: Imagine you want me to install a new chandelier in your office. You ask me to hold you harmless and indemnify you. I install the new chandelier and then it falls. Everyone escaped unharmed, except a visitor named Smith. Smith left a $1000 computer in the room and it is destroyed. Smith asks you for $1000 and you give Smith the $1000. I have agreed to make you whole (indemnify you) and so I have to give you $1000. I have also agreed to hold you harmless. This means that if this ends up being a bigger lawsuit that gets brought against you, I cannot say that it is all of your fault and has nothing to do with me. I have agreed to hold you harmless and make you whole (indemnify you) for whatever you have to spend.

Tort Liability Assumed by Contract

A general contractor might require an electrical subcontractor to sign a Hold Harmless Agreement before the subcontractor is allowed to work on a project the General Contractor is overseeing at an elementary school. The Hold Harmless Agreement might say that the subcontractor agrees to hold the General Contractor harmless and will indemnify the General Contractor for any claims of negligence associated with the subcontractor's work. The General Contractor might also be partially responsible if there is a claim and gets sued. However, by signing the Hold Harmless Agreement, the subcontractor may have agreed to assume the tort liability associated with the project.

As you can see, Tort Liability assumed by the named insured can be very broad. One could even argue that this definition alone would be sufficient to cover all of the other contracts defined.

For example: If there were no provision for a lease as an "insured contract", the landlord's contract with the tenant to indemnify and hold the landlord harmless still sounds like the named insured's contract to assume the tort liability of the landlord. I mention this because some insurance companies use their own proprietary forms and instead of having six definitions for the "insured contract", they only have one. So long as the one they keep is Tort Liability Assumed by Contract and they do not limit this in any way, there could still be substantial coverage to others provided under the "insured contract".

The importance of the "insured contract" in providing coverage extends to other areas where there is usually no coverage under the CGL policy. **For example**: Although Employer's Liability is excluded in the CGL policy, the policy states that "this exclusion does not apply to liability assumed by the insured under an "insured contract".

For example: An employer signs a lease agreement that requires the employer to hold the landlord harmless for any claims of negligence on the premises. An employee is injured when he or she slips on the premises. The employee files a worker's compensation claim against the employer. The employee also files a lawsuit against the landlord. The landlord orders the employer to hold harmless and indemnify the landlord pursuant to their lease agreement. This would be an Employer's Liability claim. This is excluded by the CGL policy unless it arises out of an "insured contract". The lease is an "insured contract" according to the CGL policy. Therefore, the employer's

CGL policy may pay for the landlord's defense because they had an "insured contract" and the exclusion for Employer's Liability does not apply to "insured contracts".

What is the Importance of an "Insured Contract" in Providing Coverage to Third Parties?

If there is bodily injury or property damage for which the named insured is obligated to pay damages by reason of the assumption of liability in an "insured contract", then the named insured's insurance policy will pay the following:

"…reasonable attorneys' fees and necessary litigation expenses incurred by or for a party other than an insured…provided [that] 1) liability to such a party for, or for the cost of, that party's defense has also been assumed in the same "insured contract" and 2) such attorney fees and litigation expenses are for defense of that party against a civil or alternative dispute resolution proceeding in which damages to which this insurance applies are alleged" (Contractual Liability Exclusion in ISO CGL Policy, CG 00 01 04 13).

I mention this as an introduction to additional insured endorsements because, instead of getting an additional insured endorsement, the entity requesting an additional insured endorsement may be better served to make sure that the named insured has sufficient limits and a properly worded "insured contract" that will pay for the third party's defense costs, attorney fees, and litigation expenses.

Think about the Caterer who wanted to cater a wedding at the hotel and the hotel required that the Caterer name the hotel as an additional insured on the Caterer's insurance policy. When we study the additional insured endorsement, we may find that there is limited coverage provided to the hotel under the endorsement.

Imagine a hotel guest gets injured as a result of the caterer's operations and the guest sues the hotel. To limit the hotel's liability in this situation, the hotel might want to name the caterer as a co-defendant in the lawsuit and establish that the caterer is the responsible party who should pay damages. If they had formed an "insured contract", the hotel could use its own legal counsel and then get reimbursed by the caterer's CGL policy. The alternative is for the hotel to rely on its coverage as an additional insured on the caterer's policy. By not having the additional insured endorsement, some attorneys feel that they are better able to represent their client's interest themselves and then seek reimbursement from the named insured's policy under the "insured contract" provision, instead of handing over their client to the named insured's insurance company for defense as an additional insured.

The CGL Additional Insured Endorsement, What is an Additional Insured Endorsement?

We mentioned above that individuals and entities can find coverage under the CGL policy as a named insured, an automatic insured, or pursuant to an "insured contract". If anyone else wants to be added as an insured on the policy, the policy needs to be endorsed to add the individual or entity as an additional insured. The additional insured endorsement changes the definition of "Who is an Insured" to include an individual or entity that otherwise may not be insured by the policy.

Why would a Named Insured want to add others as an Additional Insured?

As with just about everything in life, we tend to do something because 1) we want to do it, or because 2) we have to do it. The same is true for additional insured endorsements.

Adding Someone because you Want to Add Someone: If you are the named insured, you may want to add an individual or entity to your policy because of a special relationship that you have with the additional insured. **For example:** You may have formed a philanthropic organization that includes a number of different members. I call these people members because they have joined the organization, but they are not "members" in any sense that would provide them automatic insured status under the CGL policy. You might have a key member that helps you a great deal, is quite involved, is rather public in his/her involvement, and everyone knows this person has considerable assets. We mentioned that employees and volunteers are automatic insureds, but what if this person does not really fit these categories? What if this person is more of a consultant to this loose individually-held philanthropic organization that you have formed? This person is clearly not a named insured. This person is also not an automatic insured and there is nothing to suggest that they formed an "insured contract" for defense costs and attorney fees. If someone gets injured as a result of this organization and sues the member, the member has no rights to your CGL policy unless this friend/member is named as an additional insured. If you want your insurance policy to provide coverage for the member, you can endorse your policy so that the member is added to the policy as an additional insured.

Adding an Additional Insured because you Have to Add Someone: What is more common when it comes to adding additional insureds, is not who you want to name on the policy, but who you have to add on the policy. Every day entities around the nation require that they be named as an additional insured on someone else's policy. **For example**: A caterer wants to cater a wedding at a hotel. The hotel says that the caterer cannot come on the hotel premises until the caterer names the hotel as an additional insured on the caterer's CGL policy. Likewise, an electrician might really want to do a large job at a shopping mall and the shopping mall might require that the electrician show proof of insurance that shows the shopping mall listed as an additional insured on the electrician's policy. If you have ever worked in an insurance agency, you have no doubt heard the stress in the voice of a client who cannot get on a job or cannot get paid until the insurance company provides the required additional insured endorsement.

Practical Reasons for Someone to Request Additional Insured Status

Practical Reason 1:

Before we discuss the more accurate and academic reasons, let us talk about the real reasons why many request additional insured status. They request it because someone told them to do so. They do not understand insurance. They do not understand additional insured endorsements. They do not understand the CGL policy and its provisions to pay for the defense costs of a third-party for liability arising under an "insured contract". A risk manager just said to get the additional insured endorsement. If you are in the insurance agency world, this may mean that they will not let your client on the job or pay your client until you satisfy the request.

Practical Reason 2:

There is another practical reason why someone would require additional insured status even if they do not understand it: to provide evidence that the insurance policy really exists. This has to do with the ease of getting, or making, an evidence of coverage certificate. Forgeries happen. I was dragged into a claim once that involved a CGL evidence of coverage certificate that was signed by George Washington. I explained that no one by the name of George Washington had ever worked at the agency in question and no one by that name had ever signed certificates of insurance for the agency. Instead, what happened was that someone had forged the certificate of insurance. Thankfully, those who committed fraud changed the name so that it was clear that no one in the agency had signed it. How easy would it have been for the person who made the forgery to keep the same signature from the agency and just change the coverage dates or the coverage limits? With so many documents circulating electronically and the ease and availability of software to edit these documents, can the entity that wants to let you on the job really trust that this piece of paper that shows your limits is current and accurate? Hopefully they can trust you, but you can imagine that they would prefer to receive something from the insurance company showing that the policy has been recently endorsed to add their name on the policy as an additional insured.

Practical Reason 3:

Have you ever read the top of the standard Certificate of Liability Insurance? Most people who request to be named as an additional insured want to see themselves listed as the Certificate Holder on a Certificate of Liability Insurance with a reference that the individual or entity is named as an additional insured.

If an additional insured reads the first paragraph of the standard, Acord 25 Certificate of Liability Insurance, the additional insured might question what they are holding if the paper "confers no rights upon the certificate holder" and it "does not....amend, extend or alter the coverage." With the possibility that the certificate is a fraud (Practical Reason 2) and the realization that even an honest certificate does not extend any coverage (Practical Reason 3), you can see why someone wanting to be named as an additional insured wants an endorsement from an insurance company that proves there is a policy in place with the desired limits, and that the additional insured has been added to the policy by endorsement.

CERTIFICATE OF LIABILITY INSURANCE

DATE (MM/DD/YYYY)

THIS CERTIFICATE IS ISSUED AS A MATTER OF INFORMATION ONLY AND CONFERS NO RIGHTS UPON THE CERTIFICATE HOLDER. THIS CERTIFICATE DOES NOT AFFIRMATIVELY OR NEGATIVELY AMEND, EXTEND OR ALTER THE COVERAGE AFFORDED BY THE POLICIES BELOW. THIS CERTIFICATE OF INSURANCE DOES NOT CONSTITUTE A CONTRACT BETWEEN THE ISSUING INSURER(S), AUTHORIZED REPRESENTATIVE OR PRODUCER, AND THE CERTIFICATE HOLDER.

IMPORTANT: If the certificate holder is an ADDITIONAL INSURED, the policy(ies) must be endorsed. If SUBROGATION IS WAIVED, subject to the terms and conditions of the policy, certain policies may require an endorsement. A statement on this certificate does not confer rights to the certificate holder in lieu of such endorsement(s).

PRODUCER	CONTACT NAME:		
	PHONE (A/C, No, Ext):		FAX (A/C, No):
	E-MAIL ADDRESS:		
	INSURER(S) AFFORDING COVERAGE		NAIC #
	INSURER A :		
INSURED	INSURER B :		
	INSURER C :		
	INSURER D :		
	INSURER E :		
	INSURER F :		

COVERAGES   CERTIFICATE NUMBER: REVISION NUMBER:

THIS IS TO CERTIFY THAT THE POLICIES OF INSURANCE LISTED BELOW HAVE BEEN ISSUED TO THE INSURED NAMED ABOVE FOR THE POLICY PERIOD INDICATED. NOTWITHSTANDING ANY REQUIREMENT, TERM OR CONDITION OF ANY CONTRACT OR OTHER DOCUMENT WITH RESPECT TO WHICH THIS CERTIFICATE MAY BE ISSUED OR MAY PERTAIN, THE INSURANCE AFFORDED BY THE POLICIES DESCRIBED HEREIN IS SUBJECT TO ALL THE TERMS, EXCLUSIONS AND CONDITIONS OF SUCH POLICIES. LIMITS SHOWN MAY HAVE BEEN REDUCED BY PAID CLAIMS.

INSR LTR	TYPE OF INSURANCE	ADDL INSD	SUBR WVD	POLICY NUMBER	POLICY EFF (MM/DD/YYYY)	POLICY EXP (MM/DD/YYYY)	LIMITS	
	COMMERCIAL GENERAL LIABILITY						EACH OCCURRENCE	$
	☐ CLAIMS-MADE ☐ OCCUR						DAMAGE TO RENTED PREMISES (Ea occurrence)	$
							MED EXP (Any one person)	$
							PERSONAL & ADV INJURY	$
	GEN'L AGGREGATE LIMIT APPLIES PER:						GENERAL AGGREGATE	$
	☐ POLICY ☐ PRO-JECT ☐ LOC						PRODUCTS - COMP/OP AGG	$
	OTHER:							$
	AUTOMOBILE LIABILITY						COMBINED SINGLE LIMIT (Ea accident)	$
	☐ ANY AUTO						BODILY INJURY (Per person)	$
	☐ ALL OWNED AUTOS ☐ SCHEDULED AUTOS						BODILY INJURY (Per accident)	$
	☐ HIRED AUTOS ☐ NON-OWNED AUTOS						PROPERTY DAMAGE (Per accident)	$
								$
	☐ **UMBRELLA LIAB** ☐ OCCUR						EACH OCCURRENCE	$
	☐ **EXCESS LIAB** ☐ CLAIMS-MADE						AGGREGATE	$
	☐ DED ☐ RETENTION $							$
	WORKERS COMPENSATION AND EMPLOYERS' LIABILITY Y/N						☐ PER STATUTE ☐ OTH-ER	
	ANY PROPRIETOR/PARTNER/EXECUTIVE OFFICER/MEMBER EXCLUDED? ☐ N/A						E.L. EACH ACCIDENT	$
	(Mandatory in NH)						E.L. DISEASE - EA EMPLOYEE	$
	If yes, describe under DESCRIPTION OF OPERATIONS below						E.L. DISEASE - POLICY LIMIT	$

DESCRIPTION OF OPERATIONS / LOCATIONS / VEHICLES (ACORD 101, Additional Remarks Schedule, may be attached if more space is required)

CERTIFICATE HOLDER	CANCELLATION
	SHOULD ANY OF THE ABOVE DESCRIBED POLICIES BE CANCELLED BEFORE THE EXPIRATION DATE THEREOF, NOTICE WILL BE DELIVERED IN ACCORDANCE WITH THE POLICY PROVISIONS.
	AUTHORIZED REPRESENTATIVE

ACORD 25 (2014/01)   The ACORD name and logo are registered marks of ACORD

Substantive Reasons for Someone to Request Additional Insured Status:

Beyond the practical reasons listed above for which someone might request additional insured status, there arc five substantive reasons why someone would want additional insured status. Having additional insured status provides the additional insured with the following benefits:

1) **Money for a Hold Harmless/Indemnification Agreement**
2) **Direct Rights under the Named Insured's Policy**
3) **Protection from Subrogation**
4) **Higher Total Limits**
5) **Reduction of Insurance Costs**

1) Money for a Hold Harmless/Indemnification Agreement

A Hold Harmless Agreement is an agreement to hold someone else harmless. If you want me to sign a Hold Harmless Agreement before you allow me on your job, you are saying that you are willing to allow me on the job, but if something bad happens and you get sued, you want me to make sure that I am not going to point the finger at you and say that you were the negligent party who should pay. You want me to say it was my fault and hold you harmless for any claims that arise in connection with the job for which you are paying me.

The Hold Harmless Agreement often goes along with an Indemnification Agreement. The Indemnification Agreement is an agreement to make the other party whole. The indemnitor gives the promise to make someone else whole. The indemnitee receives the promise to be made whole. In the indemnification agreement, the indemnitor agrees to indemnify (or make whole) the indemnitee.

Using a previous example, imagine you want me to install a new chandelier in your office. You ask me to hold you harmless and indemnify you. I install the new chandelier and then it falls. Everyone escaped unharmed, except a visitor named Smith. Smith left a $1,000 computer in the room and it is destroyed. Smith asks you for $1000 and you give Smith the $1,000. I have agreed to make you whole (indemnify you) and so I have to give you $1,000.

If we change our example from a $1,000 claim to a $1 Million claim, you will understand the first reason why someone would request additional insured status. You might be pleased that I agreed to hold you harmless and indemnify you, but I have a little secret: I don't have $1 Million. Sure we wrote up the agreement, signed it, and shook hands. I feel horribly that there was a $1 Million claim arising out of my chandelier installation. I just don't have $1 Million.

When you asked me to hold you harmless and indemnify you, you probably wanted more than my willingness to exchange promises with you. You wanted money to

15

support our Hold Harmless/Indemnification Agreement in the event that something bad happens. Assuming that I have a CGL policy with $1 Million limits, the additional insured endorsement may provide the money you need to support our Hold Harmless/Indemnity Agreement.

2) Direct Rights Under the Named Insured's Policy

This is the main reason why many entities request additional insured status. When you are named as an additional insured by endorsement on someone else's policy, you become an insured on that policy with direct rights to that insurance company. Just as you might call up the insurance company on which you are a named insured, you can call the insurance company that named you as an additional insured as if it is your own personal policy. You are an insured. Looking back to the example where you hired me to install a chandelier in your office, if something goes wrong and you need to call an insurance company, you have direct rights to call my insurance company. They will recognize you as an insured if I endorsed my insurance policy to name you as an additional insured.

3) Being Named as an Additional Insured may Protect you from Subrogation

To understand this reason to request additional insured status, we have to start with a discussion on the concept of subrogation. Where one party pays the obligation of another, the party who pays has a right to go after the responsible party for reimbursement. This right to reimbursement is called subrogation. A common example of subrogation is when one insurance company goes after another insurance company for reimbursement.

For example: You hire me as a plumber to do work in your house. It turns out that I am not a particularly good plumber and now your house has extensive water damage. You file a claim against my CGL policy. My CGL insurance company says that it will be a few weeks before they can look at your house because they are reviewing a number of different construction defect claims involving contractors over the past five years. My CGL company is not saying that I am not responsible or that they will not pay. They are just letting you know that the CGL policy might not be as responsive as you would like. You can choose to walk around your soggy house in galoshes instead of slippers for weeks (or months) while my CGL policy decides what to pay, or you can call your homeowner's insurance company. Your homeowner's insurance policy may put you in a hotel or do whatever is necessary to help you according to the terms of your homeowner's insurance policy. Your insurance company will then subrogate against my insurance company. Why? I am the responsible party in this case because I am the negligent plumber. Your homeowner's insurance company is paying my obligation and they have a right to go after the responsible party for reimbursement. They will subrogate against my insurance company instead of me personally because the CGL policy is designed to cover this type of property damage caused by my operations.

To understand how being named as an additional insured can help protect you against subrogation, I need to change our example. First, before you allowed me to start work on your house, you asked me to name you as an additional insured because you already know that this is a good way to make sure that there is 1) money to support our hold harmless agreement and 2) you want direct rights to my policy. Then, before there was a flood in your house, I turned off the water to the house because I was not finished with my work. I put signs on the front door and by every faucet in the house that stated:

> # Do NOT turn on the water!
>
> # I am not finished with my job and the pipes could burst if you turn on the water.

In response, you turn on the water and the house floods.

Who is the responsible party in this story? It is you. You should not have turned on the water. Now let us pretend that my CGL policy responds immediately to this occurrence and pays $100,000 to help clean up the house. Based on the concept of subrogation, my CGL policy could then go after you, or your homeowner's insurance company, for reimbursement because my insurance company paid an obligation for which you were responsible. Why does this matter to you being named as an additional insured? Typically, insurance companies do NOT go after an insured for reimbursement. When you were added as an additional insured to my CGL policy by endorsement, you became an insured on the policy, thereby becoming someone against whom my policy would not seek reimbursement.

What is a Waiver of Subrogation?

As discussed, subrogation is the right to get reimbursed when one party pays for the obligation of another party. To waive a provision in a contract is to say that you will not enforce that provision in the contract. Therefore, a Waiver of Subrogation is a contractual agreement where one party agrees that they will not enforce their right to be reimbursed if they pay for the obligation of the other party. In the insurance context, this is a promise from one insurance company stating that they will not seek reimbursement from the insurance company of the party requiring the Waiver of Subrogation.

For example: Let us say that you hire me to do plumbing work at your house and you require that I sign a Waiver of Subrogation. Your negligence causes a water leak, my insurance company pays to clean it up, and now my insurance company wants to get reimbursed by you or your insurance company. The Waiver of Subrogation is a contractual tool that makes it explicit that my insurance company does not have a right to be reimbursed by your insurance company.

4)   Higher Total Limits

When someone gains additional insured status, they gain direct rights to the limits on the policy on which they are named as an additional insured in addition to the limits they already had on their own policy. **For example**: When you required me to name you as an additional insured on my CGL policy before I could install the chandelier in your office, you also had your own CGL policy to protect you from occurrences that could take place at your office. Both of our policies have $1 Million limits. When I named you as an additional insured on my policy, you gained direct access to my $1 Million policy limits in addition to the $1 Million policy limits on your own CGL policy. If it turns out that the Chandelier falls and creates a particularly costly claim, you have direct rights to $2 Million in policy limits.

5)   Reduction of Insurance Costs

If your insurance company has to pay claims, there is a possibility that the premiums that you pay to your insurance company will increase. If your insurance company does not have to pay claims, there is a greater likelihood that your premiums will not increase as much as they might if your insurance company does pay claims. If there is a claim that is covered by the policy that named you as an additional insured instead of your own insurance company, your insurance company does not have to pay and so it is less likely to cancel the policy or increase your premiums. Furthermore, some insurance companies for general contractors will give premium discounts to policy holders that guarantee that all subcontractors will name the general contractor as an additional insured with limits that are equal to or greater than the limits of the general contractor's policy. The general contractor's insurance policy is using this as a way to spread the risk among a number of different insurance policies. If they are sharing the exposure, they feel that they can reduce the premiums. If you rely on this to reduce premiums, make sure that all subcontractors get insurance and name the general contractor as an additional insured on the subcontractors' policies. I have seen insurance companies deny coverage to general contractors when the general contractors failed to get named as an additional insured by a subcontractor after promising his insurance company that he would be named as an additional insured by all of his subcontractors.

What is Primary and Non-Contributory Wording?

Sometimes individuals or entities request Primary and Non-Contributory Wording when they request additional insured status. This a separate endorsement that changes the CGL policy's rules on when the CGL is primary insurance, when it is excess insurance, and how it will share in the payments with other insurance companies if other insurance companies are involved.

When an insurance policy is the primary insurance policy, it will pay first. When an insurance policy is considered excess, it will not pay until the primary policy has exhausted its limits. If there are multiple insurance policies involved, they may each 1) pay equal amounts, or 2) contribute based on the "ratio of its applicable limit of insurance to the total applicable limits of insurance of all insurers" (ISO CGL Policy Section IV, Paragraph 4).

To explain these methods of sharing, imagine that you have $1 Million Limits and I have $9 Million limits. Between us, we have a total of $10 Million in limits. You have 10% of the limits. I have 90% of the limits. Now imagine that there is a $100,000 claim. If our policies share in equal amounts, each policy will pay $50,000. If our policies pay in proportion to their percentage of the total limits available, your policy will pay $10,000 (10%) and my insurance policy will pay $90,000 (90%).

The purpose of the Primary and Non-Contributory endorsement is to eliminate these methods of sharing, and make it explicit that the named insured's insurance policy will pay in full before the endorsed party's insurance will pay anything.

For example: I have a dairy and you make ice cream. I tell you that I will sell you milk, but only if you get an endorsement that shows that if both of our insurance policies are implicated, your insurance will be primary and my insurance will be excess and my insurance will NOT contribute in the sharing of the loss until your limits are exhausted. You get the endorsement and it lists me and says that, in relation to me, your insurance is primary and my insurance will not contribute.

Something goes wrong with the milk or the ice cream. We are not sure who is at fault, but it is a big claim and our insurance companies agree that they are both going to get involved. However, instead of sharing in equal parts or in proportion to my policy's percentage of the total limits available, your insurance will be primary and my policy will not contribute until you use up all of your policy limits.

Additional Insured Endorsements, Problems for the Named Insured

We have learned that the named insured may have to name someone as an additional insured to get a job, and that there are a number of reasons why someone might want to be named as an additional insured, but the named insured should be aware of five potential problems with naming others as additional insureds.

Adding an additional insured to the named insured's policy, could:

1) **Diminish the Limits Available to the Named Insured,**
2) **Unintentionally Provide Additional Coverage to the Additional Insured,**
3) **Cause Defense Conflicts, and**
4) **Cause Compliance Problems.**

1) Naming someone as an additional insured could diminish the limits available to the named insured

Adding individuals or entities to your insurance policy does not automatically increase the policy limits. Imagine that there is an electrician with $1 Million occurrence and aggregate policy limits who names someone as an additional insured to his policy every week. The electrician wants to get on the job and whoever is offering the job is requiring that they be named as an additional insured. With the electrician adding one additional insured per week, by the end of the year we have 52 different individuals or entities that have direct rights to this electrician's insurance policy. The named insured might need the $1 Million limits for an occurrence during the policy year. There are 52 other Insureds now added by endorsement that might also need the $1 Million limits for an occurrence during the policy year. If you think of the policy as a pie that could be divided into different slices, you can imagine that the slices could get pretty thin. Furthermore, if any one of the insureds has an occurrence that results in a $1 Million payment before everyone else, there is no more money available for the remaining 52 insureds.

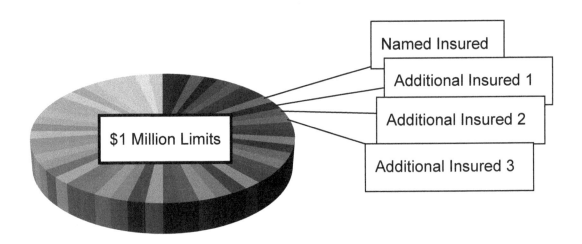

Possible Solution: Per Project Aggregate

As a way to protect against the diminution of limits caused by multiple additional insured endorsements, some additional insureds will also require that the named insured provide a Per Project Aggregate Endorsement. The Per Project Aggregate Endorsement applies the named insured's entire aggregate amount to a specifically named project. **For example**: If I am a developer building a mall and I want to hire the electrician above who names 52 different individuals or entities to his policy every year, I could have the electrician get a Per Project Aggregate Endorsement that specifically identifies my mall project. This will ensure that there will be $1 Million limits available for my project. If a named insured has $1 Million limits, and ten per project aggregate endorsements, there is the potential that the policy will pay $10 Million if the policy has to pay the full aggregate limit for each of the ten projects that are identified in their per project aggregate endorsements. You can expect that the Per Project Aggregate Endorsement usually comes at a cost, but the cost is usually not significant considering the amount of coverage being designated for a specific project. Some insurance programs will have a maximum aggregate for the endorsement. For example, a carrier might offer the Per Project Aggregate Endorsement, but limit the maximum payout per policy to $5 Million.

2) **Naming someone as an additional insured could unintentionally provide additional coverage to the additional insured**

When you add someone as an additional insured on your policy, they gain whatever benefits might come from being an insured on your policy. This can extend beyond the CGL policy on which you named the individual or entity as an additional insured.

For example: Someone wants me to name them as an additional insured on my CGL policy. I have $1 Million limits on my CGL policy. I do not particularly like or trust the person hiring me for this little job, but I can do it quickly. I do not tell them that I also have a $10 Million Excess policy that goes over my CGL policy. I figure that it does not matter and I would not want them to have rights to it anyway. What I might not realize is that the excess policy is likely to define an insured as anyone who is an insured in the underlying CGL policy. By adding this person as an additional insured to my CGL policy, I have given them not only $1 Million in CGL coverage, but potentially $11 Million in coverage because my $10 Million excess policy will treat any insured under the CGL policy as an insured in the excess policy. If you think you hid the $10 Million excess policy by not disclosing it to the person you named as an additional insured on the CGL policy, this may be true unless or until there is a claim nearing or exceeding $1 Million. At that point, the attorneys will discover the excess policy and the additional $10 Million in coverage.

3) Naming someone as an additional insured could cause defense conflicts

We hope that you get along with the people you name as an additional insured, but this usually gets tested when insurance and litigation color your relationship. Imagine that a general contractor and a subcontractor are both named as defendants in the same lawsuit and they are both being covered by the same insurance policy. The subcontractor was the named insured. The general contractor was added as an additional insured by endorsement. The general contractor might want to show that the subcontractor is completely liable in a situation as a way to establish that the general contractor is not liable at all. The subcontractor might what to show that the general contractor is completely liable as a way of showing the subcontractor is not liable at all. The defense costs are being paid—and monitored—by the same insurance company.

The subcontractor might think it is reasonable for its insurance company to pay aggressively to prove that the general contractor is at fault. The general contractor might also think that the insurance company providing it with a defense should pay aggressively to prove that the subcontractor is at fault. As you can imagine, the insurance company is going to see that when they pay aggressively to help one or both sides prove the other is responsible, they are just paying aggressively to show that one of their other insured is at fault. Whoever is at fault, they may have to pay all of the defense costs and damages. The insurance company may decide that it is cheaper to settle even if the general contractor or subcontractor think settling is unfair.

4) Naming someone as an additional insured could cause compliance problems

The entity requiring that you name them as an additional insured might have sent along a contract with various provisions. You just saw that they wanted to be named as an additional insured, and so you sent it to your insurance company or broker/agent for processing. Did you read the additional insured's requirements? Did they require that they be named as an additional insured on a certain edition of a specific endorsement?

23

Did they require that they be named for "your work", or "your ongoing operations", or "your completed operations"? Does the endorsement that you provided require that you have a written contract with the additional insured? Did the additional insured ask you to name another entity as an additional insured with which you do not have a contract? Did the additional insured require notification in the event that your policy is cancelled, non-renewed, or if there is a change of limits? Are you required to name this entity as an additional insured every year for the next 10 years or just for this year? We will cover some of these issues when we look at the individual endorsements. Be aware that by agreeing to name someone as an additional insured, you may have agreed to provide specific wording with significant coverage implications. To avoid compliance complications, you should understand the insurance requirements and endorsements so that you can ensure that you are providing (or receiving) the coverage requested.

Additional Insured Endorsements, Problems for the Additional Insured

Just as there were problems for the named insured when adding someone as an additional insured, there are problems that the additional insured must consider when being added as an additional insured. They are:

1) **Loss of Defense Control,**
2) **Limited Coverage, and**
3) **Loss of Immunity.**

1) **Being named as an additional insured may reduce your control in the defense of a claim.**

The insurance company is in charge of providing the defense offered by the policy. You may be named as an additional insured on a policy where the insurance company wants to settle the claim, and you do not. On the other hand, you may be named as an additional insured to a policy where you want the insurance company to settle the claim, and they do not. The insurance company has the right to settle even if you do not want them to settle.

For example: You own an art gallery and you get named as an additional insured to the policy of a caterer who is going to cater an event at your gallery. During the party, Paul Plaintiff, who runs a competing art gallery, says he slipped in water spilled by the caterer and sues you for $1 Million. You give the lawsuit to your caterer's insurance company and request a defense. You think the lawsuit is ridiculous. You want the caterer's insurance company to fight this lawsuit. After the insurance company assigns an attorney and the parties start exchanging letters and discovery requests, the insurance company decides that it will be cheapest to just go ahead and settle by paying Paul Plaintiff $80,000. You may not think this is right, but you do not have control of the defense.

In another example: Imagine you are a developer who was awarded a contract to build and develop a new state university campus. This contract is worth hundreds of millions of dollars to you. During development, one of your subcontractors causes $8,000 worth of property damage to a neighbor's land. In response, the neighbor sues you. You were added as an additional insured to the subcontractor's CGL policy and so you give the claim to the subcontractor's CGL policy. Your project stops and you are not allowed to continue until this issue gets resolved. The subcontractor's insurance policy wants to take time to investigate. You would prefer it if the insurance company would just pay the neighbor $8,000 so that you can continue your building project and maintain good relations with this neighbor. If you are depending on payment from the insurance company, you do not have control of the defense and you cannot tell them what claims to settle.

2)   Being named as an additional insured may provide less coverage than you expect.

There is a feeling of safety that can come with being named as an additional insured that may be unjustified. You feel like you are being responsible and now have coverage under someone else's policy, but what do you really have? You should ask the following:

> **How good is the Named Insured's insurance company,**
> **Have you read the Additional Insured Endorsement,**
> **Have you read the insurance policy, and**
> **Are you sure the Named Insured is going to maintain this coverage?**

How good is the insurance company?

When you get named as an additional insured, your coverage is only going to be as good as the insurance company's ability to stay in business and pay claims and provide a defense. As a way to ensure that the named insured has a carrier that is financially stable, some additional insureds will require the named insured to have insurance with an insurance company that has a specific credit rating or that does business in a state in a certain way. **For example**: In order for you to get a job with a large company in California, the large company may require that you name them as an additional insured with an insurance company that has an A.M. Best rating of at least A+, X, and that does business in the state on an Admitted Basis. In order to satisfy these requirements, you need to understand A.M. Best ratings and the difference between Admitted and Non-Admitted Companies.

What is an A.M. Best rating?

A.M. Best describes itself as a "global full-service credit rating agency dedicated to serving the insurance industry. It began assigning credit ratings in 1906, making it the first of today's rating agencies to use symbols to differentiate the relative creditworthiness of companies" (www.ambest.com).

A.M. Best's rating consists of a letter grade followed by a Roman numeral (e.g. A-, X). The letter grade is the *Financial Strength Rating*. The Roman numeral is the *Financial Size Category*.

A.M. Best describes the *Financial Strength Rating* as "an independent opinion of an insurer's financial strength and ability to meet its ongoing insurance policy and contract obligations. It is based on a comprehensive quantitative and qualitative evaluation of a company's balance sheet strength, operating performance and business profile" (www.ambest.com/ratings/guide.asp). This rating ends up looking like a report card for insurance companies with various insurance companies getting different grades.

For example, here are the top *Financial Strength Ratings* given by A.M. Best:

A++, A+	(Superior)	B, B-	(Fair)
A, A-	(Excellent)	C++, C+	(Marginal)
B++, B+	(Good)	C, C-	(Weak)

Whereas the above letter grades were based on evaluating an insurance company's ability to pay ongoing policy obligations, the Roman numeral that follows is a straight score that corresponds to the size of the insurance company. This number is called A.M. Best's *Financial Size Category*. This number is "based on adjusted policy holders' surplus" (APHS) and is "designed to provide a convenient indicator of the size of a company in terms of its statutory surplus and related accounts" (www.ambest.com/ratings/guide.asp).

Class	APHS ($ Millions)	Class	APHS ($ Millions)
XV	2,000 or greater	VII	50 to 100
XIV	1,500 to 2,000	VI	25 to 50
XIII	1,250 to 1,500	V	10 to 25
XII	1,000 to 1,250	IV	5 to 10
XI	750 to 1,000	III	2 to 5
X	500 to 750	II	1 to 2
IX	250 to 500	I	Less than 1
VIII	100 to 250		

Putting all of this together, what does it mean if someone gives you an insurance contract that says that you need to name them as an additional insured with a carrier that has an A.M. Best rating of at least A-, VII? It means that you need to have insurance with a company to which A.M. Best gives a *Financial Strength Rating* of at least Excellent (A-), and that has adjusted policy holders' surplus of at least $50 Million (VII). Please go to A.M. Best for a complete describe of their ratings and services.

What is the difference between an Admitted and Non-Admitted Carrier?

For this section, I am using California's admitted vs. non-admitted carrier rules as an example. If you are looking at carriers in different states, please refer to the state laws that govern how insurance companies are allowed to do business in the particular state. Insurance companies do business in California on either an admitted or non-admitted basis. Non-admitted carriers are also called surplus line insurers. If a prospective insured wants insurance with a non-admitted carrier in California, he or she is required to sign form D-1. As a way to explain the difference between admitted and non-admitted carriers, it may be helpful to look at the disclosures on form D-1.

Form D-1, Paragraph 1 informs the client that the insurance company offering the policy is "NOT LICENSED BY THE STATE OF CALIFORNIA." This sounds scary, but paragraph 7 notes that there is a list of these surplus lines insurers available on the California Department of Insurance's website. This suggests that these are real insurance companies that are allowed to do business in California. They just have decided, for whatever financial or regulatory reason, not to get licensed in California.

You can think of the California non-admitted carrier that is on the California Department of Insurance's website like someone who gets a driver's license in a state outside of California. This person did not have to pay the same fees, take the same test, or wait in the same lines as the individual with the California driver's license, but California still recognizes these out-of-state licenses and allows these drivers to travel on California's roads. The California Department of Motor Vehicles just does not keep a list of all of these drivers. When it comes to insurance, the state goes a step further and maintains a list of all of the insurance companies that are allowed to do business in California, but choose to do so without being licensed in California.

Form D-1, Paragraph 2 states that the insurer is not subject to the financial solvency regulation and enforcement that apply to California Licensed Insurers. This is related to **Paragraph 3** which informs the potential insured that the insurance company offering the **policy does NOT participate in the California Insurance Guarantee Association (CIGA).** This may make you want to ask:

What is the California Insurance Guarantee Association (CIGA)?

Admitted carriers may say that one of the benefits of going with an admitted carrier over a non-admitted carrier is CIGA. They may suggest that CIGA exists to help pay for claims in the event that an admitted carrier goes into bankruptcy, and that non-admitted carriers have no such parachute. This may be true, but just because you are with an admitted carrier that goes insolvent does not mean that CIGA is going to step in and pay or defend just like your former insurance company would have paid. As a way to explain the limited coverage offered by CIGA, it may be helpful to see what claims CIGA will not cover.

CIGA will only pay claims if they receive notice of the claim prior to the last date to file Proof of Claim with the liquidator.

When an admitted carrier goes into bankruptcy, a liquidator is assigned to process any outstanding claims. **For example**: Imagine that you are insured with Blue Insurance Company. It does business in California on an admitted basis. In 2014, it goes into bankruptcy. The liquidator of CIGA sets a Proof of Claim date of December 31, 2014. This means that CIGA will only respond to claims for which it receives Proof of Claim prior to December 31, 2014. Especially when it comes to things like latent construction defect claims, sometimes it can take a few years to learn about a claim. If you are sued for something that should be covered by this 2014 Blue Insurance Company policy, but you do not learn about it and you do not give CIGA proof of the claim until after December 31, 2014, there is no coverage from CIGA. If, on the other hand, you are able to notify CIGA prior to the last date to file the Proof of Claim, then there could be coverage.

Practically speaking, CIGA is there to protect insureds in the event that they have filed a claim with their admitted insurance company and the insurance company decides to go out of business instead of paying claims. In such a situation, the insureds would have filed their claims prior to the liquidation date, and CIGA should provide some protection to these clients if there is no other insurance available to the insureds. There would be no such parachute from an insolvent non-admitted carrier.

If you are looking at CIGA to establish which carrier you should use, remember that CIGA only helps if you end up with an insolvent carrier. Therefore, if you are looking to get insurance with unstable carriers that A.M. Best rates as C- 1, you might prefer the admitted carrier because the carriers you are considering may be heading toward insolvency. On the other hand, if you are looking at carriers that A.M. Best rates as A+, X or higher, you may not be as concerned about insolvency because you are looking at carriers that A.M. Best considers "Excellent" (A+) and have over a half a billion in adjusted policy holders' surplus (X). Again, please refer to your specific state laws for the differences between admitted and non-admitted Insurance companies in various states. (Please see The Surplus Line Association of California www.sla-cal.org for more information about the difference between California admitted vs. non-admitted carriers).

California Non-Admitted Carrier Form D-1
NOTICE

1. THE INSURANCE POLICY THAT YOU ARE APPLYING TO PURCHASE IS BEING ISSUED BY AN INSURER THAT IS NOT LICENSED BY THE STATE OF CALIFORNIA. THESE COMPANIES ARE CALLED "NONADMITTED" OR "SURPLUS LINES" INSURERS.

2. THE INSURER IS NOT SUBJECT TO THE FINANCIAL SOLVENCY REGULATION AND ENFORCEMENT THAT APPLY TO CALIFORNIA LICENSED INSURERS.

3. THE INSURER DOES NOT PARTICIPATE IN ANY OF THE INSURANCE GUARANTEE FUNDS CREATED BY CALIFORNIA LAW. THEREFORE, THESE FUNDS WILL NOT PAY YOUR CLAIMS OR PROTECT YOUR ASSETS IF THE INSURER BECOMES INSOLVENT AND IS UNABLE TO MAKE PAYMENTS AS PROMISED.

4. THE INSURER SHOULD BE LICENSED EITHER AS A FOREIGN INSURER IN ANOTHER STATE IN THE UNITED STATES OR AS A NON-UNITED STATES (ALIEN) INSURER. YOU SHOULD ASK QUESTIONS OF YOUR INSURANCE AGENT, BROKER, OR "SURPLUS LINE" BROKER OR CONTACT THE CALIFORNIA DEPARTMENT OF INSURANCE AT THE FOLLOWING TOLL-FREE TELEPHONE NUMBER: 1-800-927-4357. ASK WHETHER OR NOT THE INSURER IS LICENSED AS A FOREIGN OR NON-UNITED STATES (ALIEN) INSURER AND FOR ADDITIONAL INFORMATION ABOUT THE INSURER. YOU MAY ALSO CONTACT THE NAIC'S INTERNET WEB SITE AT WWW.NAIC.ORG.

5. FOREIGN INSURERS SHOULD BE LICENSED BY A STATE IN THE UNITED STATES AND YOU MAY CONTACT THAT STATE'S DEPARTMENT OF INSURANCE TO OBTAIN MORE INFORMATION ABOUT THAT INSURER.

6. FOR NON-UNITED STATES (ALIEN) INSURERS, THE INSURER SHOULD BE LICENSED BY A COUNTRY OUTSIDE OF THE UNITED STATES AND SHOULD BE ON THE NAIC'S INTERNATIONAL INSURERS DEPARTMENT (IID) LISTING OF APPROVED NONADMITTED NON-UNITED STATES INSURERS. ASK YOUR AGENT, BROKER, OR "SURPLUS LINE" BROKER TO OBTAIN MORE INFORMATION ABOUT THAT INSURER.

7. CALIFORNIA MAINTAINS A LIST OF ELIGIBLE SURPLUS LINES INSURERS. ASK YOUR AGENT OR BROKER IF THE INSURER IS ON THAT LIST, OR VIEW THAT LIST AT THE INTERNET WEB SITE OF THE CALIFORNIA DEPARTMENT OF INSURANCE: WWW.INSURANCE.CA.GOV.

8. IF YOU, AS THE APPLICANT, REQUIRED THAT THE INSURANCE POLICY THAT YOU HAVE PURCHASED BE BOUND IMMEDIATELY, EITHER BECAUSE EXISTING COVERAGE WAS GOING TO LAPSE WITHIN TWO BUSINESS DAYS OR BECAUSE YOU WERE REQUIRED TO HAVE COVERAGE WITHIN TWO BUSINESS DAYS, AND YOU DID NOT RECEIVE THIS DISCLOSURE FORM AND A REQUEST FOR YOUR SIGNATURE UNTIL AFTER COVERAGE BECAME EFFECTIVE, YOU HAVE THE RIGHT TO CANCEL THIS POLICY WITHIN FIVE DAYS OF RECEIVING THIS DISCLOSURE. IF YOU CANCEL COVERAGE, THE PREMIUM WILL BE PRORATED AND ANY BROKER FEE CHARGED FOR THIS INSURANCE WILL BE RETURNED TO YOU.

Date: _____

Insured: _____

Adapted from D-1 (Effective July 21, 2011). **This is NOT the official D-1. The current D-1 has the above text, but in a larger font that forces it to take two pages. A copy of the current D-1 is available at The Surplus Line Association of California (www.sla-cal.org).**

Have you read the Additional Insured Endorsement?

In addition to evaluating the strength of the insurance company, you also need to look at the strength of the additional insured endorsement. Some additional insured endorsements do not provide coverage to the additional insured once the named insured finishes the work. Other endorsements provide coverage after the named insured has completed the work, but not while the named insured is working.

For Example: Imagine you hire a mason to build a wall for you. While building the wall, the mason drops a brick on someone causing that person bodily injury. If you were named as an additional insured for "Completed Operations" and not for "Ongoing Operations," there is no coverage for you while he was building the wall. If you are sued by a party injured before the wall is completed, the mason's policy will not provide you with a defense. Similarly, if a brick falls from the wall and injures a person after the mason completes the wall and you only had coverage for the mason's "Ongoing Operations," then there is no coverage for you because the injury happened after the wall was completed and you only had coverage while the mason's operations were ongoing.

Finally, not all insurance companies or endorsements are created equally. There are additional insured endorsements that specify that the additional insured must give written notice of an occurrence to an insurance company within thirty (30) days. Other endorsements only provide coverage to the additional insured if there was a specific written contract between the additional insured and named insured. Other endorsements may state, "We have no duty to defend claims or any other liabilities arising from acts, errors or omissions of the additional insured." Maybe this would still provide a defense if the additional insured gets sued for something done by the named insured, but the additional insured should be careful about depending on additional insured endorsements for insurance protection. If you, as the additional insured, think that you have coverage because you are an additional insured, you need to read the endorsement to make sure that it does not eliminate the coverage you were expecting.

Have you read the insurance policy?

Even if you have the broadest and best additional insured endorsements that money can buy, your coverage as an additional insured will only be as good as the policy providing you with the endorsement. The additional insured endorsement makes you an insured, but it does not change the provisions on what is or is not covered by the insurance policy. You may be happy to find that you are an additional insured with a great endorsement from a highly rated insurance company, until you read the exclusions in the named insured's insurance policy.

Insurance companies may include specific exclusions to limit their risk exposure. These do not appear on the certificates of insurance or additional insured endorsement.

These additional exclusions may exclude damage from anything from work two stories above ground, to cooking with an open flame. The list of possible exclusions is endless.

For example: I have seen insurance policies sold to plumbers that excluded water damage to property caused by pipes or plumbing. Imagine that you hire a plumber to do work at your office and the plumber names you as an additional insured. The plumber causes a flood that causes $50,000 in damage to your office and $50,000 in damage to the office of the business next door. If the plumber's policy excludes water damage caused by pipes or plumbing, there would be no coverage to repair your office. Furthermore, when you get sued by the business next door and turn in a claim to get a defense, the plumber's policy will decline coverage if it contained the provision excluding water damage caused by pipes or plumbing. You need to read the named insured's insurance policy to make sure that the policy conditions or exclusions do not eliminate the coverage you were expecting.

Are you sure the named insured is going to maintain this coverage to protect you?

Let us say that you read the additional insured endorsement and it is the best and broadest ever created for someone like you. You then reviewed the named insured's insurance policy and it is providing all of the coverage you want. That is perfect, but what if the named insured cancels the policy tomorrow? You required the coverage and endorsement before this person could get the job, but what guarantees do you have that this person is going to maintain coverage? If the named insured cancels the policy or reduces the limits, how would you know? If you hire a mason to build a wall for you, do you want coverage on the mason's policy in the event that the wall falls causing bodily injury next year? (If this occurs during next year's policy, you would need to make sure that the mason gets a policy next year and continues to name you as an additional insured on next year's policy). The point of these questions is that you lose control over your insurance protection when you depend on someone else to get coverage, renew coverage, pay premiums, or maintain limits. One of the dangers to the additional insured is the false hope of coverage that may exist when you are depending on someone else for your insurance needs.

3) Being named as an additional insured may cause you to lose immunity to certain claims

Certain entities may be granted immunity by statute. **For example**: State law may grant immunity of public entities like cities. If, however, these public entities are named as an additional insured, the courts might waive immunity because there is now insurance available to pay for the defense or applicable damages instead of relying on taxpayer funds. What seemed like the responsible decision to be named as an additional insured actually removed the immunity that the entity otherwise would have enjoyed.

The Importance of Endorsement Form Numbers and Edition Dates

Additional insured endorsements come in a variety of form numbers and edition dates. The different form numbers tell you the type of endorsement. The edition date tells you when the endorsement was adopted. The difference in coverage provided by the additional insured endorsements with different form and edition dates may be significant.

For example: Let us look at **CG 20 10 11 85**.

CG	tells you that this is an endorsement for the Commercial General Liability policy
20	is the Category Number
10	is the Specific Endorsement

Together, the above describes the following endorsement:

CG 20 10 Additional Insured – Owners, Lessees or Contractors—Scheduled Person or Organization

The last four numbers are the date when the endorsement was issued.

11 85	tells you that you are looking at an endorsement that was issued in November 1985

All together, the **CG 20 10 11 85** endorsement means:

The November 1985 edition of CG 20 10 Additional Insured – Owners, Lessees or Contractors—Scheduled Person or Organization

Edition dates are important because insurance companies will use, and risk managers may require, specific endorsements for many years. Editions subsequent to the 11 85 endorsement include:

CG 20 10 11 85	From November 1985
CG 20 10 10 93	From October 1993
CG 20 10 10 01	From October 2001
CG 20 10 07 04	From July 2004
CG 20 10 04 13	From April 2013

We will see the importance of edition dates when we look at the individual endorsements. For example, editions of the CG 20 10 after 1985 do not provide coverage for completed operations or the sole negligence of the additional insured.

Standard ISO Additional Insured Endorsements

Year	Ongoing Operations	Completed Operations
1985	**CG 20 10 11 85** Who is an insured is amended to include "the person or organization shown in the Schedule, but only with respect to liability **arising out of** 'your work' for that insured by or for you." (emphasis added)	**N/A** Completed operations coverage was included under the CG 20 10 11 85.
1993	**CG 20 10 10 93** Who is an insured is amended to include "the person or organization shown in the Schedule, but only with respect to liability **arising out of** your **ongoing operations** performed for that insured." (emphasis added)	**N/A** Completed Operations coverage was eliminated under the CG 20 10 10 93
2001	**CG 20 10 10 01** Who is an insured is amended to include "[the identified persons or organizations,] but only with respect to liability **arising out of your ongoing operations** performed for that insured." (emphasis added)	**CG 20 37 10 01** **New "CG 20 13" form created to reinstate completed operations.** Who is an insured is amended to include "[the identified persons or organizations,] but only with respect to liability **arising out of** 'your work' at the locations designated and described in the [endorsement] performed for that insured and included in the **products completed operations hazard**." (emphasis added)
2004	**CG 20 10 07 04** Who is an insured is amended to include "the identified persons or organizations, "but only with respect to liability for 'bodily injury,' 'property damage' or 'personal advertising injury' **caused, in whole or in part,** by: 1. Your acts or omissions; or 2. The acts or omissions of those acting on your behalf; in the performance of your **ongoing operations** for the additional insured(s) at the locations designated [in the endorsement]." (emphasis added)	**CG 20 37 07 04** Who is an insured is amended to include "the identified persons or organizations," "but only with respect to liability for 'bodily injury' or 'property damage' **caused, in whole or in part, by** 'your work' at the location designated and described in the schedule of [the endorsement] performed for that additional insured and included in the **products-completed operations hazard**." (emphasis added)
2013	**CG 20 10 04 13** Who is an insured is defined in the same manner as in the 2004 CG 20 10 Form. However, the following language was added to the 2013 CG 20 10 Form: "The insurance afforded to such additional insured only applies **to the extent permitted by law**." (emphasis added) "If coverage provided to the additional insured is required by a contract or agreement, the insurance afforded to such additional insured **will not be broader than that which you** [the insured] **are required by the contract** or agreement to provide for such additional insured." (emphasis added) "If coverage to the additional insured is required by a contract or agreement, the most [the insurer] will pay on behalf of the additional insured is the amount of insurance: 1. **required by the contract** or agreement; or 2. **available under the applicable Limits** of Insurance shown in the Declarations; whichever is less." (emphasis added)	**CG 20 37 04 13** Who is an insured is defined in the same manner as in the 2004 CG 20 37 Form. Same limitations as noted above in the CG 20 10 04 13 Form.

SAMPLE CGL ADDITIONAL INSURED ENDORSEMENTS: CG 20 10 04 13 Additional Insured—Owners, Lessees or Contractors—Scheduled Person or Organization

This is the most common endorsement used when owners, lessees, and contractors want to be added as an additional insured on someone else's policy. Important items to know about the current edition of the CG 20 10 are the following:

1) **Importance of the name and location description**
2) **There is no coverage for completed operations (All Editions After 1985)**
3) **Liability must be caused in whole or in part by the named insured (All Editions After 2004)**
4) **The CG 20 10 04 13 only applies to the extent permitted by law (Starting in 2013)**
5) **There is no written contract requirement (All Editions)**
6) **If there is a written contract, coverage will NOT be broader than the contract (Starting in 2013)**

1) The Importance of the name and location description

As we discussed with the importance of providing the correct name for the named insured, you also need to make sure that you provide the correct name for the additional insured. If you enter the wrong entity name, there could be no coverage for the entity requiring additional insured status.

For example: Jones General Contracting wants to be named as an additional insured on Rivera Roofing's CGL policy. Jones says that they want to be named as "Jones General Contracting, Inc., Jones Project Management, LLC, and all executives, officers, and subsidiaries." In response, Rivera Roofing names "Jones General Contracting, Inc." as an additional insured. It turns out that there is bodily injury and property damage when a partially completed roof collapses. The injured parties file a lawsuit against Jones Project Management, LLC. Jones notifies the insurance company for Rivera Roofing and finds out that Jones Project Management, LLC is NOT an additional insured on the policy. Jones General Contracting, Inc. is an additional insured because they were added by endorsement. There was no endorsement adding Jones Project Management, LLC.

The box where you can enter the "Location(s) Of Covered Operations" may also prove to be an obstacle for coverage to the additional insured. If you enter a location, the additional insured status may only provide coverage for that specific location. However, if you leave this box blank, coverage may extend to all locations where the named insured conducts operations for the additional insured during the policy period.

For example: Imagine that I am a licensed contractor. You want me to build a new office for you this year on Main Street. I name you as an additional insured on my policy. I list Main Street as the address for the location on the CG 20 10 04 13. It turns out that you also have a number of residential rental properties. One day there is a water leak at one of your rentals on Third Street and you ask me to go over there and fix it. I fix it, but in the process, a pedestrian trips over the tools that I left on the sidewalk. They sue you. You turn in the claim to my insurance policy and say that you are an additional insured. You are an additional insured, but we specifically listed the Main Street address as the location on the endorsement. This occurrence took place at a location other than the location listed on the endorsement and so there may be no coverage for the incident on Third Street.

2) **There is no coverage for completed operations (All Editions After 1985)**

3) **Liability must be caused in whole or in part by the named insured (All Editions After 2004)**

Since items #2 and #3 above changed when the 1993 and 2004 editions replaced the 1985 edition, and people still request the 11 85 edition, it is helpful to discuss these provisions by contrasting the 11 85 endorsement with more recent editions.

CG 20 10 11 85 vs. later editions of CG 20 10

The CG 20 10 changed significantly after the November 1985 edition. **In the 1985 edition, additional insureds were insureds under the CG 20 10 for completed operations and the sole negligence of the additional insured. The current CG 20 10 does not cover completed operations or the sole negligence of the additional insured.**

To see how these changes took place, let us compare the wording of the 11 85 endorsement with the 04 13 endorsement:

CG 20 10 11 85

WHO IS AN INSURED (Section II) is amended to include as an insured the person or organization shown in the Schedule, but only with respect to liability arising out of "your work" for that insured by or for you.

VS.

CG 20 10 04 13

WHO IS AN INSURED is amended to include as an additional insured the person(s) or organization(s) shown in the Schedule, but only with respect to liability for "bodily injury", "property damage" or "personal and advertising injury" <u>caused, in whole or in part</u>, by:

1. <u>Your acts</u> or omissions; or
2. The acts or omissions of those acting on your behalf; in the performance of <u>your ongoing operations</u> for the additional insured(s) at the location(s) designated above.

(emphasis added)

---

2) Editions of the CG 20 10 after CG 20 10 11 85 do not have coverage for Completed Operations.

The CG 20 10 after 1985 removed completed operations when it changed coverage arising out of "your work", to coverage arising out of "your ongoing operations".

Remember that we are looking at an endorsement to the named insured's policy to add someone else as an additional insured. Since we are looking at the named insured's policy, "Your work" refers to the work of the named insured.

The CG 20 10 after November 1985 specifies that only Ongoing Operations is covered by the CG 20 10. A separate endorsement, CG 20 37 04 13 is available for Completed Operations.

One way to think of this change is to think of the endorsements like a mathematical equation where your work includes both your ongoing operations and your completed operations.

CG 20 10 04 13   **+**   **CG 20 37 04 13**   **=**   **CG 20 10 11 85**

Your Ongoing Operations   **+**   **Your Completed Operations**   **=**   **Your Work**

For example: Imagine you own a parking lot. You hire a mason to build a wall along one side of your parking lot. You have the mason name you as an additional insured on the mason's CGL policy.

The mason's ongoing operations include the time when he is working on the wall up until the time the mason completes the wall. Any liability exposure arising out of the wall after the mason completes the wall would be liability arising out of the mason's completed operations.

Occurrence # 1: Ongoing Operations

While the mason is building the wall, the mason dumps a load of bricks on top of a line of cars. This causes property damage out of the mason's ongoing operations. The car owners sue the parking lot owner.

If you were named as an additional insured using CG 20 10 04 13, there would be coverage because this is an ongoing operations exposure. This is covered under the CG 20 10 11 85 as "your work" or under subsequent editions as your "ongoing operations".

Occurrence # 2: Completed Operations

Two months after the mason finishes the wall, the wall falls on a line of cars. This causes property damage out of the mason's completed operations. The car owners sue the parking lot owner.

If you were named as an additional insured using CG 20 10 with an edition date AFTER November 1985, you will NOT have coverage for Occurrence # 2 as an additional insured on the mason's policy. Occurrence # 2 is a completed operations exposure. Versions of the CG 20 10 AFTER November 1985 specify that the additional insured is only an insured with respect to the named insured's ongoing operations.

If you were named as an additional insured using CG 20 10 11 85, you will have coverage for Occurrence # 2 as an additional insured on the mason's policy. Occurrence # 2 is a completed operations exposure. Under the CG 20 10 11 85, the additional insured is an insured with respect to the mason's work. The mason's work includes both the mason's ongoing operations and the mason's completed operations. Since the 11 85 makes the additional insured an insured with respect to the mason's work and this includes the mason's completed operations, there would be coverage to the additional insured with respect to Occurrence #2 under the CG 20 10 11 85.

(See CG 20 37 04 13 for Completed Operations).

3) Liability must be caused in Whole or In Part By the named insured.

Editions of the CG 20 10 after CG 20 10 07 04 do not have coverage for the sole negligence of the additional insured. The CG 20 10 after November 2004 removed liability arising out of the sole negligence of the additional insured when it added the requirement that the additional insured is only an insured with respect to liability "caused, in whole or in part by your acts or omissions, or acts or omissions of those acting on your behalf."

CG 20 10 11 85

WHO IS AN INSURED (Section II) is amended to include as an insured the person or organization shown in the Schedule, but only with respect to liability arising out of

"your work" for that insured by or for you.

VS.

CG 20 10 04 13

WHO IS AN INSURED is amended to include as an additional insured the person(s) or organization(s) shown in the Schedule, but only with respect to liability for "bodily injury", "property damage" or "personal and advertising injury" <u>caused, in whole or in part</u>, by:

1. Your acts or omissions; or

2. The acts or omissions of those acting on your behalf;

in the performance of your ongoing operations for the additional insured(s) at the location(s) designated above.

(emphasis added)

The elimination of sole negligence is not obvious because the CG 20 10 11 85 does not say that it will cover the sole negligence of the additional insured. It just says that it will cover liability arising out of the insured's work. You can deduce that the sole negligence of the additional insured is covered by seeing that later editions now require that the liability must be caused in whole or in part by the named insured. If the liability is caused in whole or in part by the named insured, then the additional insured could not be solely responsible.

Unlike more recent editions, additional insured endorsement CG 20 10 11 85 does not require that the named insured be solely or partially liable. However, the additional insured is still only an insured if the liability arises out of the named insured's work.

For example: Where does liability arise out of the named insured's work when the named insured is not at least partially liable?

Imagine that you own an office building and you want to hire me to install a chandelier in your conference room. You have me name you as an additional insured on my policy. I bring the chandelier to your office and get it all ready to install, but I cannot complete the safe installation of the chandelier because I am missing a part. I call you to let you know that the chandelier is safely on the ground under where I will connect it to the ceiling. I tell you that I am missing a part that is necessary for the installation and I will be back tomorrow to install it. I move all the chairs from around the chandelier and I put yellow caution tape in a circle to block anyone from walking near the chandelier. I add signs that caution everyone about the potential danger. I put a sign on the door of the conference room that says:

Danger
Do Not Enter.
The chandelier is not properly installed.
I am missing a part. I will install it properly tomorrow.

Do Not Touch the Chandelier

After I do this, you go into the conference room to inspect the chandelier. You think it looks like it would be pretty easy to install. You are able to connect it to the ceiling and it works, even without the missing part. You take down the caution signs, move the caution tape, and set up the chairs under the chandelier for a conference that you want to hold that evening. Of course, the movement of the air and activity of the room that evening causes the chandelier to fall, injuring several people. You are named in a lawsuit and you want coverage under my CGL policy.

Do you have any coverage as the additional insured on my CGL policy? This deals with a question of liability and the edition date. Remember, for the CG 20 10 11 85 endorsement, the liability only has to arise out of the named insured's work. For later editions, the liability has to be caused in whole or in part by the named insured's acts or omissions.

If you were named as an additional insured using CG 20 10 11 85, you will have coverage under my policy. It is clear from the facts that the liability arises out of my work. I brought the chandelier to the office and got it ready for installation. This is my work and liability arose out of my work.

If you were named as an additional insured using CG 20 10 with an edition date AFTER July 2004, you will NOT have coverage as an additional insured on my policy. This is because although the liability arises out of my work, the liability was not caused in whole or in part by my acts or omissions. I should not be found to be partially responsible because I made reasonable efforts to prevent the occurrence. Your actions were unforeseeable. You were solely responsible and my insurance policy should not respond.

4)   The CG 20 10 04 13 only applies to the extent permitted by law (After 2013).

The 2013 edition added the following paragraph to the CG 20 10 endorsement:

> 1. The insurance afforded to such additional insured only applies to the extent permitted by law

At first glance, this new addition may not seem important to risk managers or those wishing to be named as an additional insured because most people do not expect to have insurance beyond the extent permitted by law. However, at issue are anti-indemnification laws where some states have limited the enforceability of indemnification agreements. As discussed, indemnification is an agreement to make someone else whole. The indemnitor gives the promise to make someone whole. The indemnitee receives the promise to be made whole. In the indemnification agreement, the indemnitor agrees to indemnify (or make whole) the indemnitee.

Anti-Indemnification Laws

How these **anti-indemnification laws** relate to this updated policy language is that the contract to be named as an additional insured is viewed as a separate contract from the contract to be indemnified. Without the paragraph stating that "the insurance afforded to such additional insured only applies to the extent permitted by law," the contract to be named as an additional insured could still be enforced as a separate contract even if the indemnification agreement was void because it violated a state's anti-indemnification law (W.E. O'Neill Construction Co. v. General Casualty Co. of Illinois., 748 N.E.2d 667, 672-73 (Ill. App. Ct. 2001). When one is additional insured and receives a defense and payments from the named insured's insurance company, it can look much like the additional insured is being indemnified. The new paragraph may be an attempt to clarify that if there is a law making indemnification void, then the additional insured endorsement will also be void.

For Example: To help explain the impact of these anti-indemnification laws, imagine that the City of Los Angeles hires an independent contractor to build a school and the contractor signs a contract agreeing to indemnify the City of Los Angeles. During construction, a City of Los Angeles employee decides to use a forklift to move a pallet of materials that is in the way. This employee does not have any training on how to operate a forklift. The forklift and materials crash into a row of cars. The owners of the cars sue the City of Los Angeles because their employee was driving the forklift and their name is on signs all over the project. The City of Los Angeles tells the contractor to defend them because of their indemnification agreement. There is a problem: California has an anti-indemnification statute that prohibits indemnification agreements for injury caused solely by an indemnitee's sole negligence (Roberta Anderson, ISO's 2013 "additional insured" Endorsement Changes Merit Close Attention, 23 A.B.A. SEC. INS. COVERAGE LITIG., no. 3, May-June 2013; Cal.Civ.Code 2782(b), 2782.8). In our example, the contractor did not do anything wrong. The contractor did not drive the forklift. The employee of the City of Los Angeles drove the forklift. The city's employee damaged the cars. The City of Los Angeles is the indemnitee. The indemnification agreement should be unenforceable because the injury was caused solely by an indemnitee's sole negligence (Cal.Civ.Code 2782(b), 2782.8).

To continue this example, imagine that in addition to requiring the indemnification agreement from the contractor, the city also required that the contractor name the city as an additional insured using CG 20 10. (Imagine also that the contractor is at least partly responsible for the damage so that we can say that the liability was caused in whole or in part by the named insured, but that there was still a void indemnification agreement). Prior to the 04 13 edition, the city may still get a defense as an additional insured even though the separate indemnification agreement is void due to the state's anti-indemnification statutes (W.E. O'Neill Construction Co. v. General Casualty Co. of Illinois., 748 N.E.2d 667, 672-73 (Ill. App. Ct. 2001). When the 04 13 edition added the words "such additional insured only applies to the extent permitted by law," additional insured status may be void if the anti-indemnification statute would make indemnification void. The 04 13 edition continues to provide additional insured coverage so long as doing so does not violate an anti-indemnification statute. However, if the indemnification agreement is void due to a state's anti-indemnification statute, the additional insured endorsement is now also void because the "additional insured only applies to the extent permitted by law."

5) There is no written contract requirement (All Editions)

The standard CG 20 10 04 13 does not require a written contract. Although some insurance companies may impose this as an additional requirement, the standard wording of the endorsement does NOT require a written contract. This is a critical difference between the standard additional insured endorsements and the Blanket Endorsements discussed later. Whereas the CG 20 10 04 13 does NOT require a written contract, the Blanket Endorsement equivalent DOES require a written contract. See Blanket Endorsements CG 20 33 and CG 20 28 for a discussion on the impact of requiring a written contract.

> WARNING: If an insurance broker/agent adds the phrase "As required by written contract" this may add an additional requirement. If there is no written contract and the endorsement states that it only exists "as required by contract" then there may not be coverage for the additional insured if it was not required by written contract. Absent additional wording, the standard CG 20 10 04 13 does NOT require a written contract.

6) CG 20 10 04 13 If there is a written contract, coverage will NOT be broader than the contract (After 2013).

The 2013 edition added the following paragraph to the CG 20 10 endorsement:

> 2. If coverage provided to the additional insured is required by a contract or agreement the insurance afforded to such additional insured will not be broader than that which you are required by the contract or agreement to provide for such additional insured.

This addition to the endorsement addresses the problem of named insured's unintentionally providing additional coverage to the additional insured. As discussed, when you add someone as an additional insured on your policy, they gain whatever benefits might come from being an insured on your policy. This can extend beyond the value of the job or even beyond the limits of the CGL policy.

For example: You want to hire me to install a kitchen countertop at your house. You figure that the most damage that I could cause is $100,000, and so you require me to have insurance with limits of $100,000. It turns out that I have $1 Million limits on my CGL and another $10 Million excess policy over my CGL.

Prior to the above referenced addition to the CG 20 10, I may have inadvertently given you access not only to my $1 Million CGL policy limits, but also to my $10 Million excess policy when I named you as an additional insured on my CGL policy. Under the CG 20 10 04 13 wording, the coverage you would receive "will not be broader than that which [I was] required by the contract or agreement to provide for such additional insured." Our agreement required $100,000 in insurance coverage, and so you would only be an additional insured up to $100,000.

THIS ENDORSEMENT CHANGES THE POLICY. PLEASE READ IT CAREFULLY.

ADDITIONAL INSURED – OWNERS, LESSEES OR CONTRACTORS – (FORM B)

This endorsement modifies insurance provided under the following:

COMMERCIAL GENERAL LIABILITY COVERAGE PART.

SCHEDULE

Name of Person or Organization:

(If no entry appears above, information required to complete this endorsement will be shown in the Declarations as applicable to this endorsement.)

WHO IS AN INSURED (Section II) is amended to include as an insured the person or organization shown in the Schedule, but only with respect to liability arising out of "your work" for that insured by or for you.

THIS ENDORSEMENT CHANGES THE POLICY. PLEASE READ IT CAREFULLY.

ADDITIONAL INSURED – OWNERS, LESSEES OR CONTRACTORS – SCHEDULED PERSON OR ORGANIZATION

This endorsement modifies insurance provided under the following:

COMMERCIAL GENERAL LIABILITY COVERAGE PART

SCHEDULE

Name Of Additional Insured Person(s) Or Organization(s)	Location(s) Of Covered Operations

Information required to complete this Schedule, if not shown above, will be shown in the Declarations.

A. **Section II – Who Is An Insured** is amended to include as an additional insured the person(s) or organization(s) shown in the Schedule, but only with respect to liability for "bodily injury", "property damage" or "personal and advertising injury" caused, in whole or in part, by:

1. Your acts or omissions; or

2. The acts or omissions of those acting on your behalf;

in the performance of your ongoing operations for the additional insured(s) at the location(s) designated above.

However:

1. The Insurance afforded to such additional insured only applies to the extent permitted by law; and

2. If coverage provided to the additional insured is required by a contract or agreement, the insurance afforded to such additional insured will not be broader than that which you are required by the contract or agreement to provide for such additional insured.

B. With respect to the insurance afforded to these additional insureds, the following additional exclusions apply:

This insurance does not apply to "bodily injury" or "property damage" occurring after:

1. All work, including materials, parts or equipment furnished in connection with such work, on the project (other than service, maintenance or repairs) to be performed by or on behalf of the additional insured(s) at the location of the covered operations has been completed; or

2. That portion of "your work" out of which the injury or damage arises has been put to its intended use by any person or organization other than another contractor or subcontractor engaged in performing operations for a principal as a part of the same project.

C. With respect to the insurance afforded to these additional insureds, the following is added to **Section III – Limits Of Insurance:**

If coverage provided to the additional insured is required by a contract or agreement, the most we will pay on behalf of the additional insured is the amount of insurance:

  1. Required by the contract or agreement; or

  2. Available under the applicable Limits of Insurance shown in the Declarations;

whichever is less.

This endorsement shall not increase the applicable Limits of Insurance shown in the Declarations.

CG 20 10 04 13

"BLANKET ENDORSEMENT": CG 20 33 04 13 Additional Insured—Owners, Lessees or Contractors—Automatic Status When Required in Construction Agreement with You

The above endorsement is commonly referred to as a "Blanket" or "Automatic" Endorsement. The words "Blanket" and "Automatic" might conjure up comforting images. Maybe you are sitting on a couch under a blanket with lights programmed to automatically dim when they sense that you have fallen asleep. That sounds wonderful, but this is insurance. Don't get too comfortable and don't expect too much from your blanket endorsements.

The "Blanket" or "Automatic" endorsements are endorsements that the insurance company provides to add automatically as additional insureds, those individuals or entities for whom you are performing operations, and with whom you have agreed in writing that they would be added as an additional insured.

A positive aspect to the blanket endorsement is that insurance agencies can often send out these endorsements without specifically requesting permission from the insurance carriers. A negative aspect is the requirement that <u>there must be a written contract.</u>

Comparison:

CG 20 10 04 13	CG 20 33 04 13 (Blanket/Automatic)
Requires you to name the person/entity to be added as an additional insured	Does NOT require you to name the person/entity to be added as an additional insured
No Written Contract Requirement	Written Contract Requirement
On Going Operations Only	On Going Operations Only
No Completed Operations	No Completed Operations
Liability Caused in Whole or in Part by Named Insured	Liability Caused in Whole or in Part by Named Insured
Only to the extent of law	Only to the extent of law

Written Contract Requirement

The chief difference between the CG 20 10 and CG 20 33, is CG 20 33's requirement that there must be a written contract or agreement where the named insured has agreed to name the additional insured as an additional insured.

> **CG 20 10 04 13**
>
> "Who Is An Insured is amended to include as an additional insured the person(s) or organization(s) shown in the Schedule. . .."
>
> VS.
>
> **CG 20 33 04 13**
>
> "Who Is An Insured is amended to include as an additional insured any person or organization for whom you are performing operations when you and such person or organization have agreed in writing in a contract or agreement that such person or organization be added as an additional insured on your policy."

This may seem like a minor difference because most entities requesting additional insured status will make their request in writing. However, a closer look at contract law reveals that this requirement might mean that many who think they are additional insureds, are really not.

Privity of Contract

A basic principle of contract law is that only those who are parties to a contract receive the benefits or obligations associated with the contract. The parties to the contract are said to be in privity of contract. Any parties other than the contracting party are considered outsiders to the contract and are NOT in privity of contract.

For example: I want to sell you my book and you want to buy my book. We agree on five dollars. I am not obligated to sell you my book and you are not obligated to pay me for it. We freely exchange promises to exchange your money for my book. The contract is between us alone. We are in privity of contract. If your friend comes up to me and says, "Sell me your book for five dollars," I have no obligation to sell your friend a book because your friend was not part of our contract. Similarly, if you do not pay me, I cannot go up to your friend and say, "Pay me $5.00." This is because your friend was not part of our contract. Your friend and I are not in privity of contract and we owe each other nothing.

Problems with Privity

As a way to explain a problem with privity as it relates to additional insured endorsements, imagine that we have a custom home building project with the following parties:

1) **Owner**
2) **General Contractor**
3) **Subcontractors 1-15**

The Owner and General Contractor sign a written contract for building the house. The contract stipulated that the General Contractor must have $1 Million Limits and name the Owner as an additional insured. The contract also stipulates that all Subcontractors that the General Contractor hires must also have $1 Million Limits and name the Owner as an additional insured. The General Contractor names Owner as an additional insured on the General Contractor's CGL policy using CG 20 33 04 13 (Blanket).

The General Contractor then hires fifteen Subcontractors to help with the project. The General Contractor and each Subcontractor sign a written contract for building the house. The contract requires that each Subcontractor name the General Contractor AND the Owner as additional insured's on the Subcontractors' policies. Each Subcontractor sends the General Contractor and Owner a Certificate of Insurance and an endorsement showing Owner and General Contractor are additional insureds on the Subcontractors' CGL policies using CG 20 33 04 13 (Blanket).

The whole process was fairly painless. The Subcontractors called up their insurance agents for the endorsement. Getting the endorsement was easy because they used the blanket CG 20 33 04 13.

Where is the problem? In this example, the Owner does not have a written contract with the Subcontractors. Remember, CG 20 33 04 13 (blanket) names any person for whom you are performing operations "...**when you and such person or organization have agreed in writing in a contract or agreement that such person or organization be added as an additional insured on your policy.**" The Subcontractors have not agreed in writing with the Owner. The Subcontractors' written agreement was with the General Contractor.

Just like I cannot make your friend pay for the book that you contracted to purchase from me, the Owner cannot make the Subcontractors' insurance companies pay because of a written contract between the Owner and General Contractor. The Subcontractors are not in privity of contract with the Owner. The Subcontractors are in privity of contract with the General Contractor, and the General Contractor is in privity of contract with the Owner.

Using the scenario above, how would this have worked out if there was a massive claim and every entity seeks coverage from all possible policies?

Owner: The Owner gets coverage as an additional insured under the General Contractor's policy because the General Contractor named Owner as an additional insured per CG 20 33 04 13 and the two of them had a written contract. Even though the Owner has fifteen pieces of paper from fifteen Subcontractors saying Owner is named as an additional insured on each Subcontractor's policy, there is no coverage as an additional insured under the Subcontractors' policies because there was no written contract between the Owner and the Subcontractors, and they used endorsement CG 20 33 04 13 which requires a written contract.

General Contractor: The General Contractor gets coverage as a named insured under the General Contractor's policy. The General Contractor gets coverage as an additional insured under the fifteen Subcontractor policies because the Subcontractors named the General Contractor as an additional insured per CG 20 33 04 13, and each had a written contract with the General Contractor requiring the additional insured endorsement.

Subcontractors: The Subcontractors get coverage as the named insureds under their own individual CGL policies. They were not named as additional insureds.

How could the owner have avoided this situation?

Solution 1: Although the CG 20 33 requires a written contract, the CG 20 10 does not require a written contract. The Owner could have stipulated that the Owner was to be named as an additional insured using CG 20 10. It is not as easy as the "automatic" "blankets" of the CG 20 33, but it would have provided coverage for the Owner. Another alternative would be for the Owner to form a written contract with each subcontractor to satisfy the written contract requirement of the CG 20 33.

Solution 2: Use "Automatic" "Blanket" endorsement CG 20 38 04 13 (Discussed separately).

The CG 20 28 04 13 (blanket) shares its remaining characteristics with the CG 20 10 04 13.

> **Ongoing Operations Only**
> **No Completed Operations**
> **Liability Must be Caused in Whole or in Part by the named insured**
> **Coverage Only Applies to the Extent Permitted by Law**

For further discussion on the above remaining characteristics of the CG 20 28 04 13 (blanket), please refer to the corresponding section under the CG 20 10 04 13.

THIS ENDORSEMENT CHANGES THE POLICY. PLEASE READ IT CAREFULLY.

ADDITIONAL INSURED – OWNERS, LESSEES OR CONTRACTORS – AUTOMATIC STATUS WHEN REQUIRED IN CONSTRUCTION AGREEMENT WITH YOU

This endorsement modifies insurance provided under the following:

COMMERCIAL GENERAL LIABILITY COVERAGE PART

A. Section II – Who Is An Insured is amended to include as an additional insured any person or organization for whom you are performing operations when you and such person or organization have agreed in writing in a contract or agreement that such person or organization be added as an additional insured on your policy. Such person or organization is an additional insured only with respect to liability for "bodily injury", "property damage" or "personal and advertising injury" caused, in whole or in part, by:

1. Your acts or omissions; or

2. The acts or omissions of those acting on your behalf;

in the performance of your ongoing operations for the additional insured.

However, the insurance afforded to such additional insured:

1. Only applies to the extent permitted by law; and

2. Will not be broader than that which you are required by the contract or agreement to provide for such additional insured.

A person's or organization's status as an additional insured under this endorsement ends when your operations for that additional insured are completed.

B. With respect to the insurance afforded to these additional insureds, the following additional exclusions apply:

This insurance does not apply to:

1. "Bodily injury", "property damage" or "personal and advertising injury" arising out of the rendering of, or the failure to render, any professional architectural, engineering or surveying services, including:

   a. The preparing, approving, or failing to prepare or approve, maps, shop drawings, opinions, reports, surveys, field orders, change orders or drawings and specifications; or

   b. Supervisory, inspection, architectural or engineering activities.

This exclusion applies even if the claims against any insured allege negligence or other wrongdoing in the supervision, hiring, employment, training or monitoring of others by that insured, if the "occurrence" which caused the "bodily injury" or "property damage", or the offense which caused the "personal and advertising injury", involved the rendering of or the failure to render any professional architectural, engineering or surveying services.

2. "Bodily injury" or "property damage" occurring after:

a. All work, including materials, parts or equipment furnished in connection with such work, on the project (other than service, maintenance or repairs) to be performed by or on behalf of the additional insured(s) at the location of the covered operations has been completed; or

b. That portion of "your work" out of which the injury or damage arises has been put to its intended use by any person or organization other than another contractor or subcontractor engaged in performing operations for a principal as a part of the same project.

C. With respect to the insurance afforded to these additional insureds, the following is added to **Section III – Limits Of Insurance:**

The most we will pay on behalf of the additional insured is the amount of insurance:

1. Required by the contract or agreement you have entered into with the additional insured; or

2. Available under the applicable Limits of Insurance shown in the Declarations;

whichever is less.

This endorsement shall not increase the applicable Limits of Insurance shown in the Declarations.

CG 20 33 04 13

CG 20 38 04 13 Additional Insured—Owners, Lessees or Contractors—AUTOMATIC STATUS FOR OTHER PARTIES WHEN REQUIRED IN WRITTEN CONSTRUCTION AGREEMENT

CG 20 10 04 13	CG 20 33 04 13 (Blanket/Automatic)	CG 20 38 04 13 (Blanket/Automatic)
Requires you to name the Person/Entity to be added as an additional insured	Does NOT require you to name the Person/Entity to be added as an additional insured	Does NOT require you to name the Person/Entity to be added as an additional insured
No written contract Requirement	Written contract requirement	Written contract requirement
	No upstream parties	**Upstream parties**
On-going operations only	On-going operations only	On-going operations only
No completed operations	No completed operations	No completed operations
Liability caused in Whole or in Part by named insured	Liability caused in Whole or in Part by named insured	Liability caused in Whole or in Part by named insured
Only to the extent of law	Only to the extent of law	Only to the extent of law

Upstream Parties

You should notice a number of similarities between the CG 20 33, discussed previously, and the CG 20 38. The primary distinction between the two is coverage for Upstream Parties. Upstream Parties are the entities or individuals above the level where an entity is contracting. Without this endorsement, it may be difficult to swim upstream to provide coverage for upstream parties.

The CG 20 38 seeks to resolve the Privity Problem we discussed under the CG 20 33. In the CG 20 33, we analyzed a situation where an Owner hires a General Contractor and the General Contractor hired Subcontractors. The CG 20 33 requires a written contract between the named insured and the additional insured. The Owner ran into trouble because the Owner had a written contract with the General Contractor, but the Owner did NOT have a written contract with each individual Subcontractor. The Owner would not have additional insured status under the Subcontractors' policies using the CG 20 33 because the Owner did not have a written contract with them.

Unlike the CG 20 33, the CG 20 38 extends coverage to "any other person or organization you are required to add as an additional insured under the contract or agreement."

Using our example for the CG 20 33, the Subcontractors signed a contract with the General Contractor saying they would name the General Contractor and Owner as additional insureds. These Subcontractors did not sign a contract with the Owner.

There was no coverage for the Owner under the Subcontractors' policies when they used the CG 20 33 because the CG 20 33 requires a written contract between the named insured and the additional insured, and there was no contract between the Subcontractors and the Owner.

On the other hand, the CG 20 38 extends coverage to additional insureds that the named insured is "required to add as an additional insured under the contract agreement." The Owner is an organization the Subcontractors were required to add as an additional insured in their contract agreement with the General Contractor. Therefore, coverage would extend upstream to name the Owner as an additional insured under CG 20 38 even though the Subcontractors did not have a written contract with the Owner.

THIS ENDORSEMENT CHANGES THE POLICY. PLEASE READ IT CAREFULLY.

ADDITIONAL INSURED – OWNERS, LESSEES OR CONTRACTORS – AUTOMATIC STATUS FOR OTHER PARTIES WHEN REQUIRED IN WRITTEN CONSTRUCTION AGREEMENT

This endorsement modifies insurance provided under the following:

COMMERCIAL GENERAL LIABILITY COVERAGE PART

A. **Section II – Who Is An Insured** is amended to include as an additional insured:

1. Any person or organization for whom you are performing operations when you and such person or organization have agreed in writing in a contract or agreement that such person or organization be added as an additional insured on your policy; and

2. Any other person or organization you are required to add as an additional insured under the contract or agreement described in Paragraph **1.** above.

Such person(s) or organization(s) is an additional insured only with respect to liability for "bodily injury", "property damage" or "personal and advertising injury" caused, in whole or in part, by:

    a. Your acts or omissions; or

    b. The acts or omissions of those acting on your behalf;

in the performance of your ongoing operations for the additional insured.

However, the insurance afforded to such additional insured described above:

    a. Only applies to the extent permitted by law; and

    b. Will not be broader than that which you are required by the contract or agreement to provide for such additional insured.

A person's or organization's status as an additional insured under this endorsement ends when your operations for the person or organization described in Paragraph **1.** above are completed.

B. With respect to the insurance afforded to these additional insureds, the following additional exclusions apply:

This insurance does not apply to:

1. "Bodily injury", "property damage" or "personal and advertising injury" arising out of the rendering of, or the failure to render, any professional architectural, engineering or surveying services, including:

    a. The preparing, approving, or failing to prepare or approve, maps, shop drawings, opinions, reports, surveys, field orders, change orders or drawings and specifications; or

    b. Supervisory, inspection, architectural or engineering activities.

This exclusion applies even if the claims against any insured allege negligence or other wrongdoing in the supervision, hiring, employment, training or monitoring of others by that insured, if the "occurrence" which caused the "bodily injury" or "property damage", or the offense which caused the "personal and advertising injury", involved the rendering of, or the failure to render, any professional architectural, engineering or surveying services.

2. "Bodily injury" or "property damage" occurring after:

    a. All work, including materials, parts or equipment furnished in connection with such work, on the project (other than service, maintenance or repairs) to be performed by or on behalf of the additional insured(s) at the location of the covered operations has been completed; or

b. That portion of "your work" out of which the injury or damage arises has been put to its intended use by any person or organization other than another contractor or subcontractor engaged in performing operations for a principal as a part of the same project.

C. With respect to the insurance afforded to these additional insureds, the following is added to **Section III – Limits Of Insurance:**

The most we will pay on behalf of the additional insured is the amount of insurance:

1. Required by the contract or agreement described in Paragraph **A.1.;** or

2. Available under the applicable Limits of Insurance shown in the Declarations;

whichever is less.

This endorsement shall not increase the applicable Limits of Insurance shown in the Declarations.

CG 20 38 04 13

CG 20 37 04 13 Additional Insured—Owners, Lessees or Contractors—Completed Operations

This endorsement is used when owners, lessees, and contractors want to be added as an additional insured for COMPLETED OPERATIONS on someone else's policy. Important items to know about the CG 20 37 04 13 are the following:

1) **Importance of the Name and Location Description**
2) **There is no coverage for ongoing operations**
3) **No Coverage for the sole negligence of the Additional Insured.**
4) **The CG 20 37 04 13 only applies to the extent permitted by law (After 2013).**
5) **If there is a written contract, coverage will NOT be broader than contract (After 2013).**
6) **There is no written contract requirement (All Editions)**

1) Importance of the Name and Location Description

As we discussed with the importance of providing the correct name for the named insured, you also need to make sure that you provide the correct name for the additional insured. If you enter the wrong entity name, there could be no coverage for the entity requiring additional insured status. This was discussed previously for endorsement CG 20 10 04 13. For further examples, refer to the Importance of the Name and Location Description under CG 20 10 04 13.

2) There is no coverage for ongoing operations

The CG 20 10 removed Completed Operations after November 1985 when it changed from coverage arising out of "your work", to coverage arising out of your "ongoing operations." The CG 20 37 provides the Completed Operations coverage lacking from the CG 20 10 after the 11 85 edition.

As we discussed, we are looking at an endorsement to the named insured's policy to add someone else as an additional insured. Since we are looking at the named insured's policy, "Your work" refers to the work of the named insured. Editions of the CG 20 10 after November 1985 divide "Your Work" into:

Ongoing Operations and Completed Operations.

"Your Work" in the November 1985 endorsement included both "Your Ongoing Operations" and "Your Completed Operations." After November 1985, CG 20 10 provides the Ongoing Operations and CG 20 37 provides the completed operations.

CG 20 10 04 13	+	CG 20 37 04 13	=	CG 20 10 11 85
Your Ongoing Operations	+	**Your Completed Operations**	=	**Your Work**

Adapting a previous example, imagine you own a parking lot. You hire a mason to build a wall along one side of your parking lot. You have the mason name you as an additional insured on the mason's CGL policy.

The mason's ongoing operations include the time when he is working on the wall up until the time the mason completes the wall. Any liability exposure arising out of the wall after the mason completes the wall would be liability arising out of the mason's completed operations.

Occurrence # 1: Ongoing Operations

While the mason is building the wall, the mason dumps a load of bricks on top of a row of cars. This causes property damage out of the mason's ongoing operations. The car owners sue the parking lot owner.

If you were named as an additional insured using CG 20 37 04 13, there would be no coverage as an additional insured under the Mason's policy. That is because this is an ongoing operations exposure and the CG 20 37 04 13 covers only completed operations; not ongoing operations.

Occurrence # 2: Completed Operations

Two months after the mason finishes the wall, the wall falls on a row of cars. This causes property damage out of the mason's completed operations. The car owners sue the parking lot owner.

Occurrence # 2 is a completed operations exposure. The CG 20 37 04 13 names individuals and entities as additional insureds for Completed Operations. If you were named as an additional insured using CG 20 37 04 13, there would be coverage as an additional insured under Mason's policy because this was a completed operations exposure. (The CG 20 10 11 85 would also cover this because it names individuals and entities as additional insureds when it involves the named insured's "Work." "Work" includes ongoing operations and completed operations. Therefore, both the CG 20 37 04 13 (completed operations) or CG 20 10 11 85 (your work) would provide coverage for this occurrence.

(See CG 20 10 04 13 for Ongoing Operations).

3) No Coverage for the sole negligence of the additional insured.

The CG 20 37 states that the additional insured is only an insured with respect to liability **"caused, in whole or in part by your acts or omissions, or acts or omissions of those acting on your behalf."** There is no coverage for the sole negligence of the additional insured. This coverage matches the coverage under CG 20 10 04 13. Please refer to the CG 20 10 04 13's section on *No Coverage for the sole negligence of the additional insured* for further examples.

4) The CG 20 37 04 13 only applies to the extent permitted by law (After 2013).

The 2013 edition added the following paragraph to the CG 20 37 endorsement:

> 1. The insurance afforded to such additional insured only applies to the extent permitted by law

This wording matches the wording under CG 20 10 04 13. Please refer to the CG 20 10 04 13's section on *only applies to the extent permitted by law* for further examples.

The issue is that some states have passed anti-indemnification laws which limit the enforceability of these indemnity agreements. **For example**: California prohibits indemnification agreements for injury caused solely by an indemnitee's sole negligence (Roberta Anderson, ISO's 2013 "Additional Insured" Endorsement Changes Merit Close Attention, 23 A.B.A. SEC. INS. COVERAGE LITIG., no. 3, May-June 2013; Cal.Civ.Code 2782(b), 2782.8). The new paragraph may be an attempt to clarify that if there is a law making indemnification void, then the additional insured endorsement will also be void.

To help explain the impact of these anti-indemnification laws on the CG 20 37, imagine that the City of Los Angeles hires an independent contractor to build a school and the contractor signs an agreement indemnifying the City of Los Angeles. After construction, the principal of the school decides that the school would be a better learning environment if all of the walls were fish tanks instead of solid walls. The teachers and staff come in on a weekend and replace the walls with huge fish tanks. It is beautiful, but this obviously will not end well because we are talking about insurance risks. Let us just say that there is bodily injury and property damage to others as a result of this weekend remodeling project. The injured parties sue the City of Los Angeles. The City of Los Angeles tells the independent contractor to defend them because of their indemnification agreement. There is a problem: The independent contractor did not do anything wrong. The independent contractor made perfectly good walls that performed for their intended use and even their foreseeable misuse. The indemnification agreement is unenforceable because the injury was caused solely by an indemnitee's sole negligence (Cal.Civ.Code 2782(b), 2782.8).

Imagine also that the independent contractor is at least partly responsible for the damage so that we can say that the liability was caused in whole or in part by the named insured as required by this endorsement. Prior to the 04 13 edition, the City may still get a defense as an additional insured even though indemnification would not be possible due to the state's anti-indemnification statutes. This is because indemnification and being an additional insured are viewed as two separate things.

Prior to the 04 13 edition, the City may still get a defense as an additional insured even though the separate indemnification agreement would be void due to the state's anti-indemnification statutes (W.E. O'Neill Construction Co. v. General Casualty Co. of Illinois., 748 N.E.2d 667, 672-73 (Ill. App. Ct. 2001). When the 04 13 edition added the words "such additional insured only applies to the extent permitted by law," additional insured status may be void if the anti-indemnification statute would make indemnification void. The 04 13 edition continues to provide additional insured coverage so long as doing so does not violate an anti-indemnification statute. However, if the indemnification agreement is void due to a state's anti-indemnification statute, the additional insured endorsement is now also void because the "additional insured only applies to the extent permitted by law."

5) **If there is a written contract, coverage will NOT be broader than the contract (After 2013).**

The 2013 edition added the following paragraph to the CG 20 37 endorsement:

> 2. If coverage provided to the additional insured is required by a contract or agreement the insurance afforded to such additional insured will not be broader than that which you are required by the contract or agreement to provide for such additional insured.

This coverage matches the coverage under CG 20 10 04 13. Please refer to the CG 20 10 04 13's section on *If there is a written contract, coverage will NOT be broader than the contract* for further examples.

6) **CG 20 37 There is no written contract requirement (All Editions)**

Unlike the "Automatic" "Blanket" endorsements, the CG 20 37 04 13 does NOT require a written contract. If the named insured and insurance company agree to endorse the policy to add a person or entity as an additional insured to the policy, that person or entity is an additional insured. Some individual insurance companies will add wording requiring the existence of a written contract, but the standard CG 20 37 04 13 does NOT require a written contract.

WARNING: If an insurance broker/agent adds the phrase, "As required by written contract," this may add an additional requirement. If there is no written contract and the endorsement states that it only exists "as required by contract," then there may not be coverage for the additional insured because it was not required by written contract. Absent additional wording, the standard CG 20 37 04 13 does NOT require a written contract.

THIS ENDORSEMENT CHANGES THE POLICY. PLEASE READ IT CAREFULLY.

ADDITIONAL INSURED – OWNERS, LESSEES OR CONTRACTORS – COMPLETED OPERATIONS

This endorsement modifies insurance provided under the following:

COMMERCIAL GENERAL LIABILITY COVERAGE PART
PRODUCTS/COMPLETED OPERATIONS LIABILITY COVERAGE PART

SCHEDULE

Name Of Additional Insured Person(s) Or Organization(s)	Location And Description Of Completed Operations

Information required to complete this Schedule, if not shown above, will be shown in the Declarations.

A. **Section II – Who Is An Insured** is amended to include as an additional insured the person(s) or organization(s) shown in the Schedule, but only with respect to liability for "bodily injury" or "property damage" caused, in whole or in part, by "your work" at the location designated and described in the Schedule of this endorsement performed for that additional insured and included in the "products-completed operations hazard".

However:

1. The insurance afforded to such additional insured only applies to the extent permitted by law; and

2. If coverage provided to the additional insured is required by a contract or agreement, the insurance afforded to such additional insured will not be broader than that which you are required by the contract or agreement to provide for such additional insured.

B. With respect to the insurance afforded to these additional insureds, the following is added to **Section III – Limits Of Insurance:**

If coverage provided to the additional insured is required by a contract or agreement, the most we will pay on behalf of the additional insured is the amount of insurance:

1. Required by the contract or agreement; or

2. Available under the applicable Limits of Insurance shown in the Declarations;

whichever is less.

This endorsement shall not increase the applicable Limits of Insurance shown in the Declarations.

CG 20 11 04 13 Additional Insured—Managers or Lessors of Premises

1) Modifies "Who is An Insured" to include named real estate managers or landlords of leased premises
2) Location of leased premise(s) must be identified in the endorsement
3) Coverage ceases when named insured is no longer a tenant
4) The endorsement does NOT provide coverage for the leased premises
5) There is no coverage for structural alterations, new construction or demolition
6) The CG 20 11 04 13 only applies to the extent permitted by law
7) Coverage will NOT be broader than contract

1) CG 20 11 04 13 Modifies "Who is An Insured" to include named real estate managers or landlords of leased premises

When a business leases an office, it is common for the owner of the premises to require proof of insurance and require that the tenant name the owner or property manager as an additional insured on the tenant's CGL policy. This endorsement was created to name these entities with "respect to liability arising out of the ownership, maintenance or use of that part of the premises leased to you and shown in the Schedule."

2) CG 20 11 04 13 Location of leased premises must be identified in the endorsement

The CG 20 11 04 13 specifies that this coverage is only for "that part of the premises leased to you and shown in the Schedule." This creates a two-part test:

a) There is a LEASE, and
b) The leased premise(s) is (are) SHOWN in the endorsement

a) There is a LEASE

When the endorsement states that it is only for "that part of the premises leased to you," it implies that there must be a lease. If someone is occupying an area without a lease, this endorsement is not activated. In addition to the existence of a lease, the endorsement specifically excludes "any 'occurrence' which takes place after you cease to be a tenant in that premise." This establishes that the additional insured endorsement is only effective when the named insured is leasing a premise, and only for that period of time when the premise is being leased.

For example: Imagine a photography business rents a facility for one year. They name the landlord as an additional insured using CG 20 11 04 13. During that year, the photography business changes some electrical sockets to meet their needs. The electrical sockets are perfect for the low voltage lights they are using, but using larger voltage light bulbs in the sockets could start a fire. After the lease expires, a new tenant moves into the premise. The new tenant installs different light bulbs and this causes a fire. The landlord contacts the photography business's CGL policy and asks for coverage as an additional insured per CG 20 11 04 13. There is no coverage for the landlord because coverage ceased when the lease ended.

b) The leased premise(s) is (are) SHOWN in the endorsement.

The additional insured only achieves additional insured status if the premise in question is shown on the endorsement. This is a situation where a landlord may not achieve additional insured status because of an administrative oversight.

For example: Imagine that a tenant rents one unit of a four-unit strip mall. The tenant signs a lease and names the Landlord as an additional insured using CG 20 11 04 13. The endorsement identifies the Leased Premises as Suite A. It turns out that business is going well for the tenant and the tenant needs more space. The landlord and tenant add an addendum to the lease so that the tenant now leases suites A and B. One of the tenant's customers slips and falls in Suite B, and sues the landlord. The landlord contacts the tenant's CGL insurance company. The insurance company informs the landlord that there is no coverage for the landlord because there is only coverage for "that part of the premises leased to you and shown in the endorsement." Suite A is shown in the endorsement. Suite B is not shown in the endorsement. The endorsement does not provide coverage for the slip and fall that took place in Suite B because Suite B was not listed on the endorsement.

Insurance Practice Tip: To avoid the issue above, some insurance professionals identify the location as the "Leased premises stated in the lease." The idea is that the landlord is likely to get a lease (and rent) for any new locations that the tenant might lease during the policy period, even if they do not tell their insurance agent/broker. Another option is to list the premise address without identifying suite numbers. This could broaden the definition of the scheduled location to support coverage for expansion into adjacent suites. The effectiveness of these tips depends on the respective insurance company's requirements for identifying locations.

---

3) Coverage ceases when named insured is no longer a tenant.

The endorsement makes it clear that the endorsement does NOT provide coverage for any occurrence that takes place after the named insured is no longer a tenant of the premises. **For example**: Imagine that you own a building and you rent a suite in the building to a children's day care center. At the end of the lease, the children's day care center moves out of your building. They take out their furniture, but they leave some toys strewn across the now empty suite. You hire a real estate agent to show the suite to potential new tenants. A potential new tenant walks into the suite with the real estate agent. The potential new tenant likes to walk barefooted and learns a lesson that many parents of small children have learned: it is not a good idea to walk barefooted into a dark room filled with legos and jacks. The person who was once a potential tenant, is now a potential plaintiff, seeking to sue you for having a dangerous building that caused the potential tenant bodily injury. Even though the dangerous condition arises out of the former tenant's exposure, there is no coverage for the landlord under CG 20 11 because coverage for the landlord ceased when the named insured ceased to be a tenant. Although the day care center example is designed to be humorous, you can imagine that former tenants could leave everything from dangerous manufacturing equipment to medical instruments that could create hazardous conditions for which there is no coverage after the lease expires under the CG 20 11.

4) The Endorsement does NOT provide coverage for the leased premises

When looking at this endorsement, it is important to remember that coverage for the additional insured is not broader than the coverage provided to the named insured. The additional insured endorsement changes "Who is an Insured." It does NOT change what is covered by the policy. The standard CGL policy specifically excludes "Property Damage to Property you own, rent, or occupy." This endorsement is NOT insuring damage to the property being rented. It is insuring liabilities to third parties that could arise out of the named insured's "ownership, maintenance or use of that part of the premises leased to you and shown in the Schedule."

5) There is no coverage for structural alterations, new construction or demolition

There is no coverage for structural alterations, new construction, or demolition by the named insured. This is true even if the tenant really damages the premises or if it will be very costly for the landlord to return the premises to the condition they were in prior to the tenant.

6) The CG 20 11 04 13 only applies to the extent permitted by law.

The 2013 edition added the following paragraph to the CG 20 11 endorsement:

> 1. The insurance afforded to such additional insured only applies to the extent permitted by law

This addition matches the wording of the CG 20 10 04 13. For an explanation, please refer to the CG 20 10 04 13's section entitled, "*The CG 20 10 04 13 only applies to the extent permitted by law.*"

7) CG 20 11 04 13 Coverage will NOT be broader than contract.

The 2013 edition added the following paragraph to the CG 20 11 endorsement:

> 2. If coverage provided to the additional insured is required by a contract or agreement the insurance afforded to such additional insured will not be broader than that which you are required by the contract or agreement to provide for such additional insured.

The endorsement goes on to state that **"the most we will pay on behalf of the additional insured is the amount of insurance:**

1)   **Required by the contract or agreement; or**
2)   **Available under the applicable Limits of Insurance shown in the Declarations; whichever is less."**

These words address the problem named insured's face of unintentionally providing additional coverage to the additional insured. As discussed, when you add someone as an additional insured on your policy, that person or entity gains whatever benefits might come from being an insured on your policy. This can extend beyond the value of the premise or even beyond the limits of the CGL policy.

For example: A tenant might rent a beach shack for the tenant's surfboard rental business. The landlord requires coverage of $100,000. It turns out that the tenant has $1 Million limits on the tenant's CGL policy and another $10 Million excess policy over the CGL.

Prior to the 2013 adjustments to the CG 20 11, the tenant may have inadvertently given the landlord access not only to the tenant's $1 Million CGL policy limits, but also to the tenant's $10 Million excess policy when the tenant named the landlord as an additional insured. With the adjustments to the CG 20 11 in 2013, coverage now **"will not be broader than that which is required by the contractor or agreement to provide for such additional insured."** The agreement required $100,000 in insurance coverage, and so the landlord is only an additional insured up to $100,000.

THIS ENDORSEMENT CHANGES THE POLICY. PLEASE READ IT CAREFULLY.

ADDITIONAL INSURED – MANAGERS OR LESSORS OF PREMISES

This endorsement modifies insurance provided under the following:

COMMERCIAL GENERAL LIABILITY COVERAGE PART

SCHEDULE

Designation Of Premises (Part Leased To You):
Name Of Person(s) Or Organization(s) (Additional Insured):
Additional Premium: $

Information required to complete this Schedule, if not shown above, will be shown in the Declarations.

A. Section II – Who Is An Insured is amended to include as an additional insured the person(s) or organization(s) shown in the Schedule, but only with respect to liability arising out of the ownership, maintenance or use of that part of the premises leased to you and shown in the Schedule and subject to the following additional exclusions:

This insurance does not apply to:

1. Any "occurrence" which takes place after you cease to be a tenant in that premises.

2. Structural alterations, new construction or demolition operations performed by or on behalf of the person(s) or organization(s) shown in the Schedule.

However:

1. The insurance afforded to such additional insured only applies to the extent permitted by law; and

2. If coverage provided to the additional insured is required by a contract or agreement, the insurance afforded to such additional insured will not be broader than that which you are required by the contract or agreement to provide for such additional insured.

B. With respect to the insurance afforded to these additional insureds, the following is added to **Section III – Limits Of Insurance:**

If coverage provided to the additional insured is required by a contract or agreement, the most we will pay on behalf of the additional insured is the amount of insurance:

1. Required by the contract or agreement; or

2. Available under the applicable Limits of Insurance shown in the Declarations;

whichever is less.

This endorsement shall not increase the applicable Limits of Insurance shown in the Declarations.

CG 20 28 04 13 Additional Insured—LESSOR OF LEASED EQUIPMENT

1) **Modifies "Who is An Insured" to include owners of leased equipment**
2) **The endorsement does NOT provide coverage for the equipment leased**
3) **Coverage ceases when lease ends**
4) **Liability must be caused in whole or in part by the named insured**
5) **If coverage is required by contract, coverage will NOT be broader than the contract**
6) **No written contract requirement**

1) CG 20 28 04 13 Modifies "Who is An Insured" to include owners of leased equipment.

If someone is going to lease equipment to someone else, it is common for the owner of the equipment to require proof of insurance and require the person renting the equipment to name the owner as an additional insured on the renter's CGL policy. The type of equipment leased can range from the long-term lease of laboratory equipment, to a one-day lease of a projector for a presentation.

The endorsement states that the entity identified is an insured, **"but only with respect to liability…caused in whole or in part, by your maintenance, operation or use of equipment leased to you by such person(s) or organization(s)."** The endorsement, then, is not asking for a schedule of what you are leasing, but the name of the individual or entity you are naming as an additional insured.

For example: If you rent all of the equipment necessary to operate your pharmaceutical laboratory from Pharma Rents, Inc., you would just need to identify "Pharma Rents, Inc." as the additional insured and not all of the individual equipment that you may be renting from Pharma Rents, Inc. Of course, if your insurance company requires a schedule of all equipment rented before they will provide the endorsement, you would need to comply with your insurance company's requirements to get the endorsement. However, the endorsement wording only requires the identity of the individual or entity to be named as an additional insured.

2) The Endorsement does NOT provide coverage for the equipment leased

When looking at this endorsement, it is important to remember that coverage for the additional insured is not broader than the coverage provided to the named insured. The additional insured endorsement changes "Who is an Insured." It does not change what is covered by the policy. The standard CGL policy specifically excludes "Property damage to property you own, rent, or occupy." This endorsement is NOT insuring damage to the property being rented. It is insuring liabilities to third parties that could arise out of the named insured's "operation or use of equipment leased."

69

For example: If I rent a $5,000 copier from a copier company, the copier company may want proof that I will pay them up to $5,000 if I damage their copier. This endorsement does NOT provide this coverage. In order to provide this coverage, I would need to purchase a policy that would provide coverage for the copier. The CGL policy may pay for bodily injury or property damage to others caused by the copier, but it will not pay for the copier.

Imagine that I rented the $5,000 copier from you and named you as an additional insured per CG 20 28 04 13. I make some adjustments that I think will make the copier faster, and soon paper starts spraying out of the copier like water from a hose. Everyone in my office runs for cover. The copier then explodes. The good news is that everyone is okay. The bad news is that the copier exploded, flew through the air, and caused $100,000 in damage to the building next door where it landed. You own the copier and the owner of the building next door wants you to pay $100,000 for damages caused by your copier. You contact my insurance company for a defense. The CG 20 28 04 13 may help defend or pay the $100,000 of damage to others caused by the copier, but it will not pay $5,000 to replace your copier because the CGL policy excludes property damage to property I am renting, and I was renting your copier.

3) CG 20 28 04 13 Coverage ceases when the lease ends

CG 20 28 04 13 specifies that "this insurance does not apply to any "occurrence" which takes place after the equipment lease expires."

For example: Imagine that I rent a tractor for a day from an equipment rental business. I return the tractor at the end of the day and my lease is finished. It turns out that I did not park the tractor very well and I did not set the brake. It is on a hill overlooking a new car dealership. My negligent parking causes the tractor to roll down a hill and damage a number of different cars. The equipment dealer contacts my insurance company. They are listed as an additional insured per CG 20 28 04 13 and the property damage was caused at least in part to my **"operation or use of equipment leased."** However, there is no coverage because the occurrence took place after the equipment lease expired.

4) CG 20 28 04 13 Liability must be caused in whole or in part by named insured

The CG 20 28 states that the additional insured is only an insured with respect to liability **"caused, in whole or in part by your maintenance, operation or use of equipment leased to you by such person(s) or organization(s)."** We discussed the importance of the "caused in whole or in part" wording under the CG 20 10. This means that there is no coverage for the sole negligence of the additional insured.

Sole negligence means that one person is responsible for the entire tort of negligence. **For example:** Imagine that I rent a large tractor from Equipment Rents, LLC. The tractor says, "Equipment Rents, LLC" on the side of the tractor. I lose control of the tractor and I damage some cars parked next to my project. The owners of the cars sue Equipment Rents, LLC. Equipment Rents, LLC should enjoy additional insured status under my policy because I named them as an additional insured on my policy and the liability was caused in whole or in part by my operation of the equipment leased.

The tractor is fine after this accident and so I keep it on the job site to use the next day. I lock up the tractor when I go home for the night. I have a security guard and security cameras on the lot where I lock up the tractor. That night, someone breaks into the lot, ties up my security guard, and takes the tractor for a joy ride through town. This causes significant damage around town. A number of people file claims against Equipment Rents, LLC because that was the name on the tractor. Equipment Rents, LLC contacts my insurance company for a defense as an additional insured. There would be no coverage because the liability was not caused in whole or in part by me. I was not negligent in my operation or maintenance of the equipment. I was not negligent in parking or securing the tractor. I locked up the equipment and provided reasonable security. Since the liability was not caused in whole or in part by me, there would be no additional insured coverage for Equipment Rents, LLC.

5) **CG 20 28 04 13 If coverage is required by contract, coverage will NOT be broader than the contract**

The endorsement states that **"the most we will pay on behalf of the additional insured is the amount of insurance**:

1) **Required by the contract or agreement; or**
2) **Available under the applicable Limits of Insurance shown in the Declarations; whichever is less."**

These words address the problem named insured's face of unintentionally providing additional coverage to the additional insured. As discussed, when you add someone as an additional insured on your policy, they gain whatever benefits might come from being an insured on your policy. This can extend beyond the value of the job or even beyond the limits of the CGL policy.

For example: You might require that I have $100,000 in coverage and name you as an additional insured before you will let me rent your tractor. It turns out that I have $1 Million limits and a $10 Million excess policy over my CGL. When you learn that you are getting sued for millions of dollars because I caused serious damage while driving your tractor, you may be disappointed to learn that this policy will only pay the limits required by the contract or the limits of insurance...whichever is less. If we signed a contract requiring me to have $100,000 in coverage, you only have access to $100,000.

71

6) CG 20 28 04 13 No written contract requirement

Although it is common to have a written rental agreement when renting equipment, the written agreement is not necessary to establish additional insured status under CG 20 28 04 13.

For example: Imagine that we orally agree that I am going to rent your office copier for two months, and then I call my insurance agent/broker to request that you get added as an additional insured per CG 20 28 04 13. We have the endorsement, but we do not have a written contract. You then get sued because I plugged your copier into an outlet and somehow this caused the building next door to explode. You should have protection as an additional insured under my policy because the property damage was caused in whole or in part by my maintenance, operation, or use of the equipment.

THIS ENDORSEMENT CHANGES THE POLICY. PLEASE READ IT CAREFULLY.

ADDITIONAL INSURED – LESSOR OF LEASED EQUIPMENT

This endorsement modifies insurance provided under the following:

COMMERCIAL GENERAL LIABILITY COVERAGE PART

SCHEDULE

Name Of Additional Insured Person(s) Or Organization(s):

Information required to complete this Schedule, if not shown above, will be shown in the Declarations.

A. **Section II – Who Is An Insured** is amended to include as an additional insured the person(s) or organization(s) shown in the Schedule, but only with respect to liability for "bodily injury", "property damage" or "personal and advertising injury" caused, in whole or in part, by your maintenance, operation or use of equipment leased to you by such person(s) or organization(s).

However:

1. The insurance afforded to such additional insured only applies to the extent permitted by law; and

2. If coverage provided to the additional insured is required by a contract or agreement, the insurance afforded to such additional insured will not be broader than that which you are required by the contract or agreement to provide for such additional insured.

B. With respect to the insurance afforded to these additional insureds, this insurance does not apply to any "occurrence" which takes place after the equipment lease expires.

C. With respect to the insurance afforded to these additional insureds, the following is added to **Section III – Limits Of Insurance:**

If coverage provided to the additional insured is required by a contract or agreement, the most we will pay on behalf of the additional insured is the amount of insurance:

1. Required by the contract or agreement; or

2. Available under the applicable Limits of Insurance shown in the Declarations;

whichever is less.

This endorsement shall not increase the applicable Limits of Insurance shown in the Declarations.

"BLANKET ENDORSEMENT": CG 20 34 04 13 Additional Insured— LESSOR OF LEASED EQUIPMENT—AUTOMATIC STATUS WHEN REQUIRED IN LEASE AGREEMENT WITH YOU

1) Modifies "Who is An Insured" to include owners of leased equipment
2) Coverage ceases when lease ends
3) Coverage will NOT be broader than the contract
4) Liability must be caused in whole or in part by the named insured
5) Written contract requirement

The "Blanket" or "Automatic" endorsements are endorsements that the insurance company provides to add individuals or entities as additional insureds automatically when there is a written contract.

A positive aspect to the blanket endorsement is that insurance brokers and agents can often send these endorsements quickly without specifically requesting permission from the insurance carriers. A negative aspect is the requirement that there must be a written contract.

CG 20 28 04 13	CG 20 34 04 13 (Blanket/Automatic)
Requires you to name the Person/Entity to be added as an additional insured	Does NOT require you to name the Person/Entity to be added as an additional insured
No written contract requirement	Written contract requirement
Coverage ceases when lease ends	Coverage ceases when lease ends
Liability caused in whole or in part by named insured	Liability caused in whole or in part by named insured
Coverage will not be broader than contract	Coverage will not be broader than contract

Since items 1-4 of the CG 20 34 are identical to items previously discussed in the CG 20 28, please refer to the appropriate section under the CG 20 28 for more details.

5) Written Contract Requirement

The chief difference between the CG 20 28 and CG 20 34 is CG 20 34's requirement that there must be a written contract or agreement where the named insured has agreed to name an entity or individual as an additional insured.

CG 20 28 04 13

"Who Is An Insured is amended to include as an additional insured the person(s) or organization(s) shown in the Schedule..."

VS.

CG 20 34 04 13

Who Is An Insured is amended to include as an additional insured any person(s) or organization(s) from whom you lease equipment when you and such person(s) or organization(s) have agreed in writing in a contract or agreement that such person(s) or organization(s) be added as an additional insured on your policy"

This above distinction may seem like a minor difference because most entities requesting additional insured status will make their request in writing. However, in addition to the privity problems discussed under CG 20 33 04 13, there is also the practical problem that comes with familiarity and laziness. The privity problems discussed in CG 20 33 04 13 match the privity problems of the CG 20 34 04 13. Please refer to the section on Privity Problems under Section CG 20 33 04 13 for more details on privity.

The good thing about needing a written equipment rental agreement is that many equipment rental places print their rental agreements on their receipts. You may think you are at the cash register to get a receipt, but the receipt often has extra words about holding the equipment rental place harmless. This is obviously in writing and they make you sign it before you can leave with the equipment. This may be a written contract for the purposes of this endorsement.

If a contractor rents frequently from the same equipment rental place, the equipment rental place may want to have an additional insured endorsement on file from the contractor's CGL policy. If you use the CG 20 34 04 13, you do not need to name the equipment rental place. The only requirement is that there is a written contract between the named insured and the additional insured, and they have one of these every time the contractor signs the receipt.

The problem comes with familiarity and laziness. **For example:** A contractor signed a rental agreement for a small wheeled tractor to work on a drainage ditch. The contractor thought it would just take one day to finish the job. It is at the end of the day and it starts to rain. The contractor returns the small wheeled tractor because he needs to get the larger tractor with crawler treads. It is closing time at the equipment rental place and it starts raining harder. The equipment rental place is trying to get equipment out of the rain and they have already closed the cash register for the day. The contractor states, "I need to rent a big tractor now or my project will flood."

They yell back and forth to each other through the rain and agree that the contractor can take the larger tractor with crawler treads. They will create the receipt and payment tomorrow.

We have a situation where the equipment rental place has additional insured endorsement CG 20 34 04 13, but there is no written agreement for renting the larger tractor. There was a written agreement for the smaller tractor, but that agreement ended when the contractor returned it.

By now you also know that the story will not end well because we need an example where the equipment rental company gets sued and needs to call the contractor's insurance company for a defense. Even though the owner of the tractor has an additional insured endorsement in hand, there is no coverage for the tractor owner because they used CG 20 34 04 13 (Blanket). CG 20 34 04 13 (Blanket) requires a written contract and in this situation, there was no written contract for the big tractor. If they would have used CG 20 28 04 13, specifically naming the equipment rental place, then there would be additional insured status because the CG 20 28 04 13 does NOT require a written contract. Since they chose to use CG 20 34 04 13 (Blanket) which requires a written contract, and they did not have a written contract, there is no coverage for the equipment owner.

Other than the written contract requirement, the terms of the CG 20 34 04 13 (blanket) match the terms of the CG 20 28 04 13. Please refer to the section on the CG 20 28 04 13 for a description of the terms shared with the CG 20 34 04 13 (blanket).

THIS ENDORSEMENT CHANGES THE POLICY. PLEASE READ IT CAREFULLY.

ADDITIONAL INSURED – LESSOR OF LEASED EQUIPMENT – AUTOMATIC STATUS WHEN REQUIRED IN LEASE AGREEMENT WITH YOU

This endorsement modifies insurance provided under the following:

COMMERCIAL GENERAL LIABILITY COVERAGE PART

A. **Section II – Who Is An Insured** is amended to include as an additional insured any person(s) or organization(s) from whom you lease equipment when you and such person(s) or organization(s) have agreed in writing in a contract or agreement that such person(s) or organization(s) be added as an additional insured on your policy. Such person(s) or organization(s) is an insured only with respect to liability for "bodily injury", "property damage" or "personal and advertising injury" caused, in whole or in part, by your maintenance, operation or use of equipment leased to you by such person(s) or organization(s).

However, the insurance afforded to such additional insured:

1. Only applies to the extent permitted by law; and

2. Will not be broader than that which you are required by the contract or agreement to provide for such additional insured.

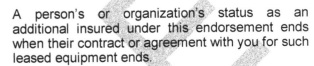

A person's or organization's status as an additional insured under this endorsement ends when their contract or agreement with you for such leased equipment ends.

B. With respect to the insurance afforded to these additional insureds, this insurance does not apply to any "occurrence" which takes place after the equipment lease expires.

C. With respect to the insurance afforded to these additional insureds, the following is added to **Section III – Limits Of Insurance:**

The most we will pay on behalf of the additional insured is the amount of insurance:

1. Required by the contract or agreement you have entered into with the additional insured; or

2. Available under the applicable Limits of Insurance shown in the Declarations;

whichever is less.

This endorsement shall not increase the applicable Limits of Insurance shown in the Declarations.